Friedrich Hirth

Notes on the Chinese Documentary Style

Friedrich Hirth

Notes on the Chinese Documentary Style

ISBN/EAN: 9783337004446

Printed in Europe, USA, Canada, Australia, Japan

Cover: Foto ©ninafisch / pixelio.de

More available books at **www.hansebooks.com**

文件字句入門
Wên - Chien   Tzŭ - Chü   Ju - Mên

NOTES

ON THE

CHINESE DOCUMENTARY STYLE.

By F. HIRTH, Ph.D.,

*Deputy Commissioner and Assistant Statistical Secretary,
Inspectorate General of Customs, Shanghai.*

Kelly & Walsh, Limited:
Shanghai, Hongkong, Yokohama, and Singapore.

1888.

PREFACE.

THE selection of notes embodied in these pages, which owe their origin to the liberal encouragement of SIR ROBERT HART, K.C.M.G., Inspector General of Customs, has been compiled for the purpose of stimulating students of the Chinese business style in making a systematic study of the rules governing this branch of the written language. In conceiving this idea about fifteen years ago, the author was chiefly indebted to the sudden progress he made in grasping the sense of a Chinese text on having simply worked himself through the pages of Stanislas Julien's *Syntaxe Nouvelle de la Langue Chinoise*. It seemed to him at the time that, under the guidance of this ingenious work, he had learned more of the real spirit of the language in a few weeks than had been the case in as many months during which he was left to his own imagination in pursuing his studies by mere practice, and that the benefits thus derived in respect of the ancient written language might be brought to bear, with greater advantage to the practical student, on the modern documentary style. The author has since had no reason to regret his grammatical efforts, and although many of his own friends can boast of wonderful attainments in the knowledge of written Chinese by mere routine, he is deeply convinced of the fact that every hour invested in systematic study will, in the long run, save several hours which it will be necessary to spend in routine work, in order to realise by instinct the force of the various grammatical phases of the style.

In offering to students some of his observations, the author wishes it to be understood that his work does not replace a complete grammar, but that its chief object is to persuade the reader to make grammatical observations himself and to gradually lead him into the habit of tracing the rule where rule exists. To obtain this end, a study of the rules governing the *Ku-wên*, or ancient style, under the guidance of Julien's *Syntaxe*, or Prof. von der Gabelentz's *Chinesische Grammatik* (Leipzig, 1881), will be highly useful, since the spirit of Chinese grammar is the same now as it was in ancient times, the differences referring to detail rather than to principle. Grammatical hints will also be found in Part II. of the author's *Text Book of Documentary Chinese*, which should be regarded as a supplement to the present volume.

Students having managed the spoken language to a certain extent, and being able to express their thoughts fluently, frequently get disgusted with the difficulties of the written language and are only too ready to take refuge in that *pons asinorum*, the native writer, who will interpret the sense of difficult passages in plain colloquial without being able to analyse the construction of even the simplest sentence. The greater command they have over the spoken language, the easier they will find it to have such difficulties explained to them without being able to judge themselves. The danger of becoming thus dependent upon the intelligence of a native assistant is obvious, and cases in which a student who has done good work because he has enjoyed the benefit of having a clever

Hsien-shêng at his side, finds himself suddenly in great distress when he has to work with a less intelligent man or without any such help at all, are too frequent to need any further comment. The student should, therefore, in good time become accustomed to use his eyes, instead of his ears, in reading Chinese; and, in order to attain this end, I would advise him to commence studying the colloquial and the written Chinese at the same time, taking either branch in hand separately and just as seriously as though he were going to study two difficult languages like Latin and Greek. His progress in the spoken language will thus be less rapid than if he devote himself to colloquial studies entirely for the first two or three years; but he will be less liable to discouragement when called upon to exert himself in the written language, decidedly the more difficult branch of his studies.

As to the latter, I would recommend him to begin by reading and translating, without a native teacher, but with the assistance of the Vocabulary in Volume II., the first 43 documents in Vol. I. of the Text Book, checking the sense of his own version with the translations contained in the Appendix of Vol. II. After this he should proceed in the same manner with Wade's "Documentary Course," up to, say, Document No. 57, being careful to study all the notes contained in the "Key," and consulting the Dictionary in preference to the native teacher. At this stage he will be sufficiently prepared to commence systematic studies, and he should devote a certain time every day to reading these Notes, which have been so arranged as to give him as little work with the Dictionary as possible. If by this means he contract a taste for making grammatical observations himself, by collecting examples of an analogous character in order to find the rule governing each mode of expression which may be new to him, the object of this publication will be best fulfilled.

How to continue his studies thereafter will be a question of individual need. The "Documentary Course" and the "Text Book" will furnish him ample material for home study, and the student in China will soon find there is no lack of opportunity for practice in the routine of daily life.

SHANGHAI, *February*, 1888.

TABLE OF CONTENTS.

	PAGE
Introduction	1
Grammatical Agents	11
Purality and Totality	17
Numeral Phrases	24
Reduplication	25
Pural by 等 têng	25
,, ,, 類 lei and 輩 pei	28
該 kai and 所有 so-yu	29
The numeral 一 i representing the definite article	33
The Subject	34
由 yu, introducing the logical subject	36
The Object	39
將 chiang, a sign of the Object	40
把 pa and 以 i, as signs of the Object	42
The phrase 以 i... 為 wei,	43
惟 wei... 是 shih,...	47
The Genitive, Anteposition, 之 chih,	48
The Dative	64
Pronouns, Personal	68
,, Demonstrative	74
,, Reflexive	83
,, Reciprocal	85
,, Relative	85
,, Distributive	93
,, Indefinite	94
同 t'ung and 異 i	94
一 i, One, expressing sameness	95
他 t'a, ALIUS	97
Numerals	98
Adjectives	111
The Comparative	115
The Superlative	121
Negatives	124
Adverbs	138
Prepositions : 在 tsai and 於 yü,	143

INTRODUCTION.

The documentary language or business style, as T. T. MEADOWS calls it, is that style of the Chinese written language which is generally used in all kinds of documents public and private. If we except novels, poetry and certain essays distinctly meant to be written in the ancient or archaic style, it may be said that it is the written language of the day; in fact the modern prose of China; for everything written by the ordinary Chinese has a businesslike character. There can be no doubt that the style adopted by native writers in the Chinese newspapers published in Shanghai and Hongkong is much nearer the style used in official despatches than it is to the language of the Four Books, of Ma Tuanlin, or of any of the Dynastic Histories; not to speak of the *Peking Gazette*, the only really indigenous periodical published in the Empire, which indeed contains papers written in the business style exclusive of all others.

T. T. MEADOWS, on p. 13 of his *Desultory Notes*,* justly remarks: "M. RÉMUSAT, in his *Grammaire Chinoise*, notices three styles of the Chinese language, which he calls, *style antique, style littéraire*, and *langue des magistrats*, or *langue mandarinique*; but he is not quite correct in his definitions of these, and he altogether overlooks what I call the *business style* of the Chinese written language, classing the works and documents in which it is found, partly with those

---

* "*Desultory Notes on the Government and People of China*, etc." London, 1847.

which form specimens of the *style antique*, and partly with those in which something like the *langue mandarinique*, or spoken language, is found."

The same omission may be noticed in all grammatical works on the Chinese language now existing, from PREMARE down to ENDLICHER, SCHOTT and JULIEN,* whose works chiefly describe the *Ku-wên* or ancient style, with occasional remarks on the modern spoken language. Julien, in the introduction to his *Syntaxe Nouvelle de la Langue Chinoise*, says with regard to his work: "Ce n'est point, à proprement parler, une grammaire chinoise complète dans toutes ses parties; c'est seulement un supplément considérable à toutes celles qui ont paru jusqu' à ce jour." His book is no doubt a considerable supplement to all the preceding grammars; still it supplements only their rules of the classical language and completely ignores the style of the present day.

If we consider the importance of this branch of Chinese literature, we cannot but wonder why *vis-à-vis* the profuse grammatical studies made by European scholars in the ancient written and the modern colloquial styles, nobody has as yet undertaken to prepare something approaching a digest of the rules distinguishing it from the style of Chinese commonly cultivated by Foreign grammarians. The business style is certainly studied by more individuals than the ancient language and, apart from the scientific interest one may take in the knowledge of its rules, deserves for this reason alone to be described in its grammatical phases.

It is not likely that a digest of the grammatical rules governing the business style will be a very important means

---

* When these notes were written, VON DER GABELENTZ' exhaustive grammar was not published yet. I need hardly say that, since it is distinctly stated to be written "mit Ausschluss des niederen Stiles," the business style is as yet not represented amongst Chinese grammatical works.

of acquiring its knowledge as compared with the more practical use of a chrestomathy and a dictionary. Yet it may be hoped that it will be a welcome study not only to those who take a merely theoretical interest in the structure of the language, but also an encouragement to the practical student. It appears that the day is not far distant when, for most palpable, because practical reasons, the knowledge of the business style will be regarded as of equal importance with that of the *Ku-wên*; time will, therefore, call forth scientific works on the laws governing this, as it did in the case of the ancient, style. The notes that follow are intended to throw out some of the main features of such a work. Their object will in the first instance be the establishment of a number of rules without attempting anything approaching a system. Many of these rules are, of course, closely related to those governing the Chinese language in general, while others are especially characteristic of the business style. It is this latter class of rules which are here chiefly cared for.

The collection of rules here given is, however, far from being exhaustive, and must be looked at as a nucleus of grammatical experiences to which every student should add his own,—as the acquirement of the habit of searching for analogies in reading sentences of a similar turn will soon enable him to do.

To describe the general features of the documentary language as distinguished from other styles Mr. Meadows' observations from the second of his *Desultory Notes* will be found the best introduction.

" That which I call *business style*," he says, "deserves to be particularised as such, because a very distinct and easily definable line of demarcation may be drawn between it and the other styles of the Chinese language, and because, as will be shown below, it is for, by far, the greater number of foreigners the most useful to know. The ancient style is so sententious and concise as to become vague, so that several of the best specimens of it, as, for instance, "The Four Books," cannot be understood by the Chinese themselves without an explanation, either written or verbal, *to each new passage*. It contains, too, a great number of the characters denominated hsü, *empty*, by the Chinese, the influence of which in sentences it is extremely difficult for Europeans to discern. Now the business style, though sharing in the peculiar conciseness of the Chinese language, as compared with those of Europe, has always so much diffusiveness, that any man who has made such progress as enables him to read one or two works in that style, will find no difficulty in reading an entirely new work composed in it. He may occasionally have to apply to his dictionaries for the meaning of a new term, but the style will no longer be a difficulty. There is generally nothing superfluous in it; it is terse, but it is not so concise as to be vague. In the business style the hsü, or empty characters, noticed above, are scarcely ever used; in which particular it differs, not only from the ancient style, but also from the *style littéraire* or *wên-ch'ang*—a term that the Chinese apply almost exclusively to the compositions of the candidates at examinations, and others of a similar nature. The business style differs from the *wên-ch'ang* in another material point. In the latter, an appropriate and well understood term, which does not suit the rythmus, is exchanged for one less suitable in sense and not so well defined, but which sounds better; in the business style, on the other hand, little or no attention is paid to the rythmus or sound, but distinctness being the chief object in view, a word or term is repeated again and again, whenever its omission would appear likely to cause ambiguity. From the spoken language the business style, like every other written style, differs very widely. As a vast number of the Chinese words which are written quite differently are pronounced exactly alike, they are obliged in speaking to join others to them, in order to be understood; just as if we were obliged, in *speaking* English, to say : sky-sun, child-son ; sacred-holy, all-wholly ; only-sole, spirit-soul; ocean-sea, look-see, &c. &c.; although there is no mistaking the words sun and son, holy and wholly, soul and sole, sea and see, &c. when *written*. Now in speaking English it is really not necessary, because our homophonous words are so few, that the context always leads the mind of the hearer to the particular word meant. Nearly the whole of the Chinese spoken language is, however, composed of double words, or compounds (formed in a manner similar to the above, or in some other manner, but always with the same object); and these are either not used at all in writing, or only one of their constituent parts is used. The above, and some other differences, reach to such an extent, that the Chinese colloquial, or spoken language, and the business style are, so far as the task of acquiring them is concerned, really two different languages. When we learn French, in learning to speak it we at the same time learn to read it; but learning the best spoken Chinese and learning to read the written language, is like learning to speak the Parisian French and learning to read Latin. *This is one cause of the great difficulty of learning the Chinese;* for the man who has completely mastered the spoken language, and can read the same language when written, is *literally* as far from being able to read a book composed in comparatively simple business style, as a man who can speak French on all subjects fluently, and read what he speaks when written, is from being able to read the simplest Latin book; in other words, he is unable to read a single paragraph of it.

"The business style is that used in statistical works, in the *Ta-ching hui-tien* (the collected statutes of the empire), and in the Penal and other codes. It is also used in the addresses of high mandarins and the Boards at Peking to the Emperor, and in the edicts and rescripts of the latter (hence the Peking Gazette is entirely written in this style); further, in all the proclamations and notifications of the mandarins; in their official correspondence with each other; in petitions from the people to the mandarins, and the answers of the latter; in judicial decisions, bailbonds, warrants, permits, passports, &c. &c.; in leases, and deeds of transfer of landed property between private parties; and in all mercantile-legal papers, as contracts for the performance of work, or for the purchase of goods, promissory notes, and bills of exchange.

"In some of the old statutes contained in the *Ta-ching hui-tien*, and that old part of the Penal Code to which Sir George Staunton chiefly confined himself in his Translation, the business style is very terse, resembling in so far, the ancient style; but there it distinguishes itself from the latter, by a total want of empty particles, of which it contains a few in other specimens. It is necessary to remark, however, that there are some histories composed in a style apparently a mixture of the ancient and the business style; and that there are many works which it would be difficult to assign to any one style.

"There is still another style which deserves to be noticed, and which, for the sake of distinction, I shall call the *familiar style*. It lies between the business style and the colloquial, and is that in which light works, such as novels, plays, &c. are composed; for it must be observed, even the Chinese plays and the dialogues in novels do not form strictly correct examples of the actually spoken language. The reason is, that much of what is used in the spoken language is not only unnecessary to express the same idea on paper, but would, as useless verbiage, rather cause obscurity; just as it would render the English obscure if we were to write sky-sun, child-son, &c. when the words sun and son are of themselves sufficiently distinct. The style in plays is, however, a near approach to the actual spoken language, and even the narrative in novels contains a great admixture of it.

"To recapitulate: the *ancient style* is sententious, so concise as to be vague and unintelligible without explanations; contains a great number of the difficult *hsü* or empty particles, but does not confine itself by a strict attention to the rythmus. The best specimens of it are to be found in the ancient classics, the works of Confucius and of the philosophers of the same school. The Chinese say of this style, that it is *very profound*.

"The *wên-ch'ang*, or *literary style*, is sufficiently diffuse to be intelligible, contains a great number of the empty particles, and conforms strictly to the rythmus. The compositions of the literary graduates at the examinations are almost the only specimens of this style, all compositions in which are characterized by a constant reference to a theme or text. The Chinese say of this style, that it is *very abstract*.

"The *business style* is always sufficiently diffuse to be intelligible; it always contains few, many specimens of it none, of the empty particles; and it does not confine itself by any attention to the rhythmus. Works on government and statistics, and the laws, are comprised in this style; and all documents of a legal nature, all official correspondence on business, are written in it. The Chinese say of this style, that it is *plain and distinct*.

"The *familiar style* is the least terse of any of the Chinese written styles; it contains very few of the empty particles, it does not confine itself by any attention to the rhythmus, and contains a considerable admixture of terms used in the spoken language.

"The narrative parts of novels form examples of this style, which the Chinese designate as *plain but shallow.*

"The *colloquial Chinese* (referring to the general oral language of the country, as spoken by the mandarins, not to any of the dialects) is the least terse style in the language; it contains no characters that can fairly be classed with those called empty, and in it, of course, not the slightest attention is paid to the rhythmus.

"Plays and the dialogues in novels are written in a style nearly resembling the colloquial Chinese, and sentences precisely the same as those used in oral conversation occur not unfrequently in such writings; but I have never seen any continuous piece in the exact spoken language.

"The above enables us to form an opinion as to the proper style to study. Missionaries may, possibly, find it useful to study the ancient style, in order to acquaint themselves with Chinese ethics in the original language. But every moment that the government servant or the merchant spends in the study of the ancient style, is altogether misemployed. I mention this because it is very much the custom in Europe to commence the study of the language with the classical " Four Books," a work that is entirely written in the ancient style. Now a man may, doubtless, with the assistance of a translation and explanations, go through the whole of the " Four Books," and render himself, in a great measure, master of the original. But this would be a task to him who commenced with that classic of at least a couple of years of unremitting study; and when he had finished it, he would be totally unable to make a correct translation of the simplest official letter or mercantile contract. A thorough knowledge of the "Four Books" in the original is, too, as useless to the man who wishes to translate business papers from English into Chinese, as it is to him who wishes to translate similar papers from Chinese into English; for, even supposing him able (a *very* bold supposition) to compose in the style of that work, the want of business terms would offer an insuperable difficulty; and if he were to finish his task by borrowing these from a dictionary, the Chinese would probably not understand what he had written, so concise and vague is the ancient style. In short, for the British officer or merchant to study the "Four Books," with a view of making a practical use of what he learns, is rather more absurd than it would be for the mandarin or the Chinese merchant to study Proverbs and Ecclesiastes, with the view of writing to, and drawing up their agreements with the English in the style of these books.

"The first business of the foreign government agent or merchant, who intends studying the Chinese, is to learn to speak, which can be best done by reading some work in the *familiar style*, as a play or novel, with a good teacher, paying, however, still more attention to the language the latter uses in conversation, than to that contained in the books. When the student is able to converse with some degree of ease, and can understand the explanations of his teacher, he should commence reading the more easy compositions in the business style, as the proclamations of local mandarins, contracts, &c.; and as he gradually progresses in his knowledge of the language, proceed to read the Peking Gazette, and the various books which are enumerated above as being written in the business style."

I have quoted Mr. MEADOWS' chapter on the business style almost at full length, because the majority of readers will not act an the simple reference to another book, and because the passage quoted contains the best introduction to a branch of Chinese literature which even at the present time is not sufficiently recognised as an independent style of writing. The details distinguishing it from other styles will help to bear out the correctness of Mr. MEADOWS' general sketch.

It is a matter of course that examples, necessary to illustrate the grammatical rules should be selected from documents written in that style, just as nearly all the examples of our Chinese grammars of the ancient language are derived from the classics and cognate works, while grammars of the Mandarin colloquial quote from novels written in that dialect. Of documents written in the business style there is, of course, no lack. These notes are, however, with the exception of occasional quotations from other sources, confined to examples contained in Wade's Documentary Course* for more than one reason. In the first instance, it will often be necessary to make the reader acquainted with the whole context of a long period, which it would be tedious to quote at full length, in order to prove a certain grammatical rule; in such cases it will suffice to refer to such and such a page in Wade's Collection, which may be assumed to be in the hands af every student of the business style.

---

* 文件自邇集 *Wên-chien Tzŭ-êrh chi*, a series of Papers selected as specimens of Documentary Chinese, with key, by Thomas Francis Wade, C. B. London, 1867, 2 Vols., 4°, Trübner & Co. I understand that a considerable number of copies of this valuable text book are still on the market.

NOTES.

GRAMMATICAL AGENTS.

(1). MARSHMAN, on p. 194 of his *Clavis Sinica*, says: "A Chinese character may in general be considered as conveying an idea without reference to any part of speech; and its being used as a substantive, an adjective, or a verb, depends on circumstances." The circumstances upon which thus the grammatical standing of a character depends may be said to be of a twofold nature. They may be due

1. to its *position*, *i.e.* the order in which it occurs when compared with other characters; or
2. to the influence of certain other characters occurring in the same sentence, which, for the sake of convenience, I shall call *auxiliary characters*.

Such auxiliary characters either precede or follow the one affected by them, and may be separated from it by one or more indifferent characters; they may be properly said to perform the service of prefixes and suffixes, and replace to some extent the inflection of Western languages.

A great many grammatical relations may, in Chinese, be simply expressed by *position;* here indeed more than in any other language it is by position that a word receives its peculiar force. The addition of other characters modifying its grammatical sense, though in many cases a necessity, is frequently but a mere luxury, somewhat approaching that prodigal use of grammatical organs by which Aryan and Semitic tongues are distinguished from the Chinese and its cognate languages.

Speaking of this kind of luxuries, Sanscrit appears to be the most extravagant, English the most economical of Indo-German languages; Greek, Latin and Gothic may be called profuse in the use of forms when compared to modern Greek, the Romance, and the modern Teutonic languages; nay, the history of almost every existing Western language shows a tendency to gradually move from extravagance to economy with regard to the use of forms. In the Chinese written language a tendency to move in the opposite direction may be clearly observed. Here the ancient style is the simplest; in it position is still the reigning element. As we go through the older historians and the mediæval encyclopedists, down to the edicts and memorials of the present dynasty, a gradual decay of the ancient simplicity marks the effect of time, and step by step it may be traced how position makes room to the use of auxiliary characters.

In spite of all this Chinese is still a most economical language if we look at the grammatical organs at its disposal, so much so that there is no lack of scholars who earnestly believe there is not such a thing as grammar at all in Chinese.

This may be true to those who are under the impression that a grammar must necessarily be a book showing the declension of nouns and the conjugation of verbs. But if grammar is at all what the name implies, the "art of writing," the art of writing any language must be based upon grammar; I mean that a language, written or spoken, cannot be understood, unless it be based upon certain conventional rules. The knowledge of these conventional rules is taught in the grammar of the language. We may even go farther and say,—whatever the system of a language may be, inflective or monosyllabic, the *principles* of grammar must be the same in all languages, because speech is nothing but thought rendered perceptible by the senses. The rules of thought, however, are not accidental, but deeply rooted in human nature; they are taught by the science commonly called logic. Therefore, the principles of grammar, the logic of human speech as it were, must be inherent in every language. It is just as impossible to *think*, as it is to *say*, "the dog bites the boy," without the idea of a subject (dog), a verb (bites) and an object (boy). MARSHMAN is, therefore, right in making the following observation: "The language of every country must possess words which denote *things* and others which signify *qualities*. It must have words to express *actions done;* and these as done by one or many; already done, now doing, or intended to be done; they must also be described as done absolutely or conditionally, as proper to be done, or peremptorily commanded. Further the various circumstances of the *doer*, and of the *subject* of the action, must also be either plainly expressed or tacitly understood; hence the need of prepositions *connecting* words, too, necessarily exist in every language, as well as those which express the *emotions* of the mind. Thus the principles of grammar must substantially exist in every language."

And they do exist in Chinese. But the manner in which they are expressed greatly deviates from that traditional form in which our western minds are trained. With regard to this it has been already remarked that *position* and the use of *auxiliary characters* are the two principal agents at the disposal of the language.

Position, in Chinese, acts in a similar way as, though on a much larger scale than, position in English, where, to choose a most striking example, there is no formal distinction made between the nominative and accusative cases. The subject, in English, must precede the object, and the verb usually stands between the two. Position has in this case become a necessity, and under certain circumstances the simplest sentence could not be understood without it, owing to the absence of inflection. "The son beats the father," and "the father beats the son," in these two sentences the words "son" and "father" receive their particular force as subject and object respectively merely by position. Where suffixes exist position usually ceases to be binding, because it is no longer the only agent for expressing grammatical differences. In Latin, for instance, we are free to render "the son beats the father" by "filius verberat patrem," "patrem verberat filius," "verberat patrem filius", or "verberat filius patrem," without being misunderstood. It appears that here position loses its influence because other means to express the principles of grammar are at hand. Such other means appear in the Aryan languages either in the shape of certain changes made on a certain word (inflection), or in the addition of certain other words. "I do" and "I shall do," is an example of another word being added.

It is the addition of other words (*auxiliary characters*) that, wherever the agency of position is given up, is resorted to in the Chinese language, which I need scarcely remark is destitute of all inflection. It is just this point which many cannot reconcile with the idea of any grammatical rule in Chinese, who if we speak of cases are bound to think of *mensa, mensæ*, etc., or of *amo, amavi*, etc., when tenses are alluded to.

If, with other foreign writers on Chinese grammar I retain the technicalities of Western grammar, it is not only for the practical reason put forth by Julien who (*Syntaxe Nouvelle*, p. 9) simply declares his inability of treating upon the subject from his point of view, without this "conventional language," but chiefly because I look at them as a sort of philosophical necessity, the principles of thought peculiar to the human mind rather than to any particular language. Speaking, therefore, of the Verb Passive, for instance, I do not mean to show how the "Passive" is formed in Chinese, but simply answer the question : what are the means at the disposal of the language for expressing that change taking place with an active verb which in Western language is expressed by giving it the passive form ?

The above refers to Chinese in general, and applies to the various spoken dialects as well as the written language. *Position* and the use of *auxiliary characters*, it has been shown, are the two grammatical agents of the language in general. In the written language, more especially, a third class of influences greatly affects the grammatical bearing of sentences which, different though they are in nature, we may comprise in the general name of *symmetry*. It shows itself in a certain predilection of writers to use for certain terms,* or for certain sentences, or clauses, a fixed number of characters, as often as the corresponding class of terms, sentences, or clauses occur within a certain section.

Nearly every term is represented in Chinese by a monosyllabic *and* a bisyllabic expression, so as to leave it to the writer's option whether he choose the one or the other ; many even necessarily consist or may be made to consist of more syllables. Now the rule with regard to terms is that a monosyllable should match a monosyllable, a bisyllable a

---

* Following the usage adopted by grammatical writers I shall, in the course of these notes, occasionally call a Chinese character a "word;" but a "term" I mean to be the equivalent of any words of a Western language, whether represented in Chinese by one, or by more characters.

bisyllable, etc., no matter whether these terms follow each other in the same sentence, or occupy corresponding parts in two or more different sentences, whether they be in a sort of antithetical relation to each other, or merely accidentally occupy the position in which they appear.

A similar rule prevails with regard to sentences and clauses. Whole periods are constructed on the principle of symmetry, which it may be said influences the mind of Chinese writers so as to give even the run of their ideas a peculiar symmetrical turn.*

From a Western point of view this would seem to be rather a rhetorical than a grammatical peculiarity of the language. Examples approaching it may be found in

* In this respect my own exsperience is at variance with the remarks made by Mr. MEADOWS who maintains that rythm is ignored in the business style; if not resorted to so regularly as in the classical language, examples abound in all classes of documents, and I am prepared to uphold what I said formerly in connection with a riview of VON DER GABELENTZ' work, in that "too much stress cannot be laid upon what we may call a special idiom of the Chinese language,—the power of expressing logical divisions by rhythm, antithesis, and parallelism. Rhythm, which in Western languages is confined to the poetical style, plays, in Chinese, a great part even in the prosiest of prose. An ordinary notice, found on the street corners of a city in Fukien, the most trivial communication to the public, reads like a poem on account of the rhythmical arrangement of its characters. Every clause has a fixed number of characters, say four, five, six, or seven, which is an important assistance in the logical division, coinciding, as a matter of course, with grammatical pauses. Rhythm, antithesis, and parallelism are in many cases the only key to open up passages otherwise quite unintelligible. "By knowing the rules of position," says VON DER GABELENTZ [*Beitrag zur Geschichte der chinesischen Grammatiken*, in the Journal of the German Oriental Society, Vol. XXXVII. p. 605], "I know what I have to look for at the head, in the middle, and at the close of a sentence. But where can I find the beginning and the end of a sentence? Occasionally certain particles will serve as a guide. But what am I to do, if there are none—which often happens? In such cases I run my eye over the text, not caring how many unknown characters it may contain; I discover here a parallelism, there an antithesis, begin to count the number of characters being followed by the same word, and soon find the key is in my hands. You see, the proceeding is as superficial and formal as possible; the sifting of its material part follows afterwards. But what have I done, then? I have simply discovered the stylistic pattern the author has had before his mind when writing; I am beating the time before knowing the tune."

several of the great writers familiar to us even without our going back as far as the orators of ancient Rome or Greece. Although, properly speaking, not more than a sort of mannerism, affected ever since Chinese was written, it has now taken almost entire possession of the language, and may, however objectionable any pedantry of the kind would be considered when forced upon Western writers and readers, be justified in more than one way. Its principal advantage to us it would appear is the possibility it affords to at once recognise grammatical pauses, to clearly distinguish what characters are to be taken together to form a term, and what terms are to be taken together to form a sentence or a clause.

PLURALITY AND TOTALITY.

(2) Wherever the distinction between singular and plural is not essential it is left unexpressed. In most cases where Western languages have a plural it is not essential; and in such cases it is in Chinese generally inferred from the connection of the sentence. Where it has to be expressed in Chinese this may be done by the addition of a substantive meaning *class, category*, etc., or by the existence in the same sentence of a word expressing totality. The substitution of *totality* for *plurality* is most frequently resorted to whenever its expression becomes a necessity, hence a great many adjectives or pronouns meaning *all, each, every*, are often practically nothing but signs of the plural. Some of these words expressing totality are placed *before* the noun to which they apply, others again *follow* it, either immediately, or separated from it by one or more characters.

1. Characters usually preceding the noun: 諸 *chu*; 列 *lieh*; 衆 *chung*; 庶 *shu*; 多 *to*; 閤 *ho*; 凡 *fan*; 各 *ko*.

2. Characters usually placed after the noun and, therefore, having retrospective power:

皆 *chieh*; 偕 *hsieh*; 均 *chün*; 咸 *hsien*; 僉 *ch'ien*; 至 *ch'üan*; 具 *chü*; 俱 *chü*; 悉 *hsi*; 擧 *chü*; 都 *tu*; 曹 *ts'ao*.

---

(3) Of the characters preceding nouns 諸 *chu* and 各 *ko* are those chiefly used in the business style.

諸 *chu* as a sign of plurality and totality may be frequently well translated by the plural *with* the definite article, as it usually designates the class of individuals in their totality without, however, laying stress on the word "*all*." 諸領事官 *chu ling-shih-kuan* means "*the* Consuls" in so far as they form the Consular body; 諸事 *chu shih*, matters, affairs, *i.e.* all the affairs that there are; 南洋諸番 *nan-yang chu fan*, THE foreign tribes of the Southern ocean; 諸國 *chu kuo*, THE countries (315). To these I wish to compare the examples quoted by Premare: 諸說 *chu shuo*, "all opinions, whatever is said"; in ordinary context I would say "*the* opinions;" 諸儒 *chu ju*, "THE literati;" 諸家 *chu chia*, "all the families;" 諸子 *chu tzŭ* "the philosophers;" 諸侯 *chu hou* "the tributary kings."—諸位 *chu wei* and 諸君 *chu chün* are very commonly used for "the gentlemen," as 申¹ 報² 舘³ 諸⁴ 位⁵ ⁴*chu-*⁵*wei* the gentlemen of [or in charge of] ¹*Shên-*²*pao* ³*kuan* the Shên-pao (newspaper) Office. Similarly 諸¹ 先² 生³ 皆⁴ 無⁵ 病⁶ ¹ *chu* ²*hsien* ³*shêng* the teachers (are) ⁴*chieh* all ⁵*wu* not ⁶*ping* sick. 列 *lieh* is used in the same manner as 諸 *chu*.

各 *ko* on the other hand, which in ordinary Chinese chiefly represents the pronoun "each" or "every," but is quite commonly employed as a sign of the plural in the business language, expresses a totality not of a whole class, but of all the different individuals each considered by itself. We, therefore, find 各 *ko* chiefly then employed as a sign of the plural, when it is preceded by either several adjectives or genitives, or one adjective or genitive implying a plurality of qualities each of which is attributable to one of the individuals of which 各 *ko* is to designate a plurality. Examples:

文武各官 *wên wu ko kuan* the civil and military officers.

通商各口 *t'ung shang ko k'ou* the ports of foreign trade, "the Treaty ports."

約¹ 內² 各³ 條⁴—³*ko* ⁴*t'iao* the articles ²*nei* in, of ¹*yüeh* the Treaty (15).

其¹ 餘² 各³ 犯⁴—¹*ch'i* the ²*yü* remaining ³*ko* ⁴*fan* criminals (31).

氏¹ 夫² 各³ 鋪⁴ ¹*shih* my (a woman's) ²*fu* husband's ³*ko* ⁴*p'u* shops (65).

各子 *ko tzŭ* (her) sons (64; 65).

各員 *ko yüan*, officers (106).

各委員 *ko wei yüan*, the deputies (106).

The remaining characters expressing totality and placed *before* the noun are of less frequent occurence. As likely to be met with in documents I mention: 眾人 *chung jên*, men, mankind; 眾商 *chung shang* all the merchants, or the merchants; 眾生 *chung shêng* all living things, or creatures, mankind; 眾鳥 *chung niao*, the birds (as a class of the animal kingdom), as in the example: the parrot is distinguished from *chung niao*, all [other] birds [Schott]. 庶士 *shu shih* all the public officers, the scholars; 庶民 *shu min* the people, the masses; 多方 *to fang* all quarters, all directions, "les pays" (Rémusat); 多言 *to yen*, many words, etc.; 闔村 *ho ts'un* all the village, or the whole of the villages (309); 闔港周知 *ho chiang chou chih*, "the whole colony knows this" (65).

闔 *ho* has rather a collective sense.

(4) Of the characters mentioned as following the noun and being used as signs of the plural 都 *tu*, all, is peculiar to the Mandarin colloquial, while all the others are more or less frequently employed in the written language, especially in the business style. Their original meaning is *all, equally*, etc., and they act similarly as the word *all* would act were we to form two sentences in English as follows:

The sheep died; and
The sheep all died.

In the former sentence it is not shewn whether one or more sheep died, while the word *all* in the second example establishes the plurality. Now, just as in this case the word *all* may be separated from its noun, *sheep*, by several other words, as in "the sheep, on having eaten the grass, all died," without its losing the power of placing the word sheep into the plural number, all the above Chinese particles retain their retrospective force no matter whether they follow their noun immediately or are separated from it by one or more other characters. Examples:

我¹ 軍² 因³ 無⁴ 糧⁵ 食⁶ 皆⁷ 採⁸ 野⁹ 菜¹⁰ 充¹¹ 饑¹²—¹*wo* our ²*chün* soldiers, army (collective noun) ³*yin* because of ⁴*wu* not having ⁵*liang*-⁶*shih* grain-food, provisions ⁷*chieh* all (alluding to the different individuals forming the army) ⁸*ts'ai* plucking ⁹*yeh* wild ¹⁰*ts'ai* vegetables ¹¹*ch'ung* filled, satisfied ¹²*chi* (their) hunger (p. 393).

The classical example 四¹ 海² 之³ 內⁴ 皆⁵ 兄⁶ 弟⁷ 也⁸—¹*ssŭ*-²*hai*-³*chih*-⁴*nei* [those that are] within the four seas, *i.e.* all men [are] ⁵*chieh* all ⁶*hsiung*-⁷*ti* brethren (⁸*yeh* final particle), is occasionally met with in despatches treating of cosmopolitan subjects.

生¹ 意² 之³ 人⁴ 均⁵ 不⁶ 敢⁷ 來⁸ 城⁹ 買¹⁰ 賣¹¹—⁴*jên* men ³*chih* of ¹*shêng*-²*i* commerce (commercial people, merchants)

⁵*chün* all, equally ⁶*pu* do not ⁷*kan* dare to ⁸*lai* come ⁹*ch'êng* to the city ¹⁰*mai*-¹¹*mai* to trade.

田¹ 禾² 均³ 遭⁴ 淹⁵ 沒⁶—¹*t'ien* fields and ²*ho* grain ³*chün* all, equally ⁴*tsao* met with, hence a sign of the passive, "got," "were," ⁵*yen*-⁶*mo* drowned.

商¹ 賈² 來³ 歸⁴ 咸⁵ 歌⁶ 樂⁷ 國⁸—¹*shang*-²*ku* the traders ³*lai* ⁴*kuei* coming hither ⁵*hsien* all ⁶*ko* sing, praise ⁷*lê* the happy ⁸*kuo* land (p. 62).

萬 國 咸 甯 *wan kuo hsien ning* all nations enjoy peace (Premare).

臣¹ 等² 詢³ 諸⁴ 年⁵ 老⁶ 商⁷ 民⁸ 僉⁹ 謂¹⁰ etc.—¹*ch'ên*-²*têng* the ministers, "your Majesty's servants" ³*hsün* examining ⁴*chu* the (plural: τους) ⁵*nien* ⁶*lao* aged ⁷*shang* ⁸*min* merchants ⁹*ch'ien* (they) all ¹⁰*wei* said, etc. "The oldest merchants, examined by your Majesty's servants, unanimously declared, etc."

僉 *ch'ien* may in many cases be translated by "unanimously," as in this word the original force of its meaning is still more powerful than in all the others. If, e.g., the members of a guild 僉 禀 *ch'ien ping*, they mean to present an "*unanimous*" petition.

閨¹ 中² 婦³ 女⁴ 全⁵ 生⁶ 妄⁷ 想⁸—³*fu*-⁴*nü* women ²*chung* in ¹*kuei* their appartments ⁵*ch'üan* all ⁶*shêng* create ⁷*wang* reckless, idle ⁸*hsiang* thoughts.

禾¹ 苗² 俱³ 在⁴ 水⁵ 中⁶—¹*ho* ²*miao* the sprouts of grain, the paddy shoots (are) ³*chü* all ⁴*tsai* ⁶*chung* in, within ⁵*shui* the water. "The paddy shoots are covered by the flood."

所¹ 有² 香³ 港⁴ 公⁵ 務⁶ 悉⁷ 係⁸ 貴⁹ 帥¹⁰ 門¹¹ 辦¹² 理¹³—¹*so* ²*yu* ("those which there are," representing the article) "the" ⁵*kung* public ⁶*wu* affairs (of) ³*hsiang*-⁴*chiang* Hongkong ⁷*hsi* all ⁸*hsi* are ⁹*kuei* ¹⁰*chün*-¹¹*mên* by you, the General ¹²*pan* ¹³*li* managed. "All public business at Hongkong is to be administered by the General." (30).

It need hardly be mentioned that all these words expressing totality have frequently to be translated by their original meaning "all, each, equally, etc.," but in the majority of cases in which they are employed they may simply be looked at as taking the place of signs of the plural.

(5) The character — *i*, one, in connection with certain substantives,* forms adverbs having almost the same force as the above pronouns. These adverbs may in many cases be translated by *all, equally*, etc., but very frequently are merely signs of the plural or reinforce the plurality of a noun preceding them. Thus employed we find — 體 *i-tʻi;* — 切 *i-chʻieh;* — 律 *i-lü;* — 併 *i-ping;* — 概 *i-kai;* — 同 *i-tʻung;* — 齊 *i-chʻi;* and others, meaning "all taken together," "all as a body," etc.

殿¹飭² 巡³ 船⁴ 捕⁵ 役⁶ —⁷ 體⁸ 實⁹ 力¹⁰ 查¹¹ 拿¹²—to¹yen strictly ²*chʻih* order ⁵*pu*-⁶*i* the constables of the ³*hsün* ⁴*chʻuan* guard boats, to ⁷*i* ⁸*tʻi* all ⁹*shih* ¹⁰*li* with real effort ¹¹*chʻa* examine and ¹²*na* seize.

似¹ 此² 製³ 賣⁴ 處⁵ 所⁶ —⁷ 切⁸ 與⁹ 例¹⁰ 無¹¹ 礙¹² ¹*ssŭ* like ²*tzʻŭ* this, i.e. thus ⁵*chʻu*-⁶*so* the places of ³*chih* manufacture and ⁴*mai* sale (are) ⁷*i*-⁸*chʻieh* all ¹¹*wu* without ¹²*ai* difficulty ⁹*yü* with, with regard to ¹⁰*li* the law. "There is nothing, therefore, either in the place of its (gunpowder) manufacture, or in the place of its sale, that is in non-accordance with the law." (Wade, 57; for examples of *i-chʻieh* applied in similar and different ways, see pp. 15 col. 2; 26 col. 1; 111 col. 1; 118 col. 3; 368 col. 10; 371 col. 9.)

— 律 *i-lü* presupposes a plurality of subjects in so far as, by it, the action of the verb is meant to be *uniformly* attributed to them.

---

* Occasionally also standing by itself, as in the classical examples quoted by Julien on p. 155 in Vol. I of his *Syntaxe Nouvelle*.

此¹ 冊² 長³ 短⁴ 寬⁵ 窄⁶ 圖⁷ 內⁸ 一⁹ 律¹⁰ 不¹¹ 得¹² 參¹³ 差¹⁴ 不¹⁵ 齊¹⁶—³ch'ang ⁴tuan the length and ⁵k'uan ⁶chai width of ¹tz'ŭ ²ts'ê these registers ⁸nei within a ⁷t'uan "volunteer district" ⁹i-¹⁰lü uniformly ¹¹pu ¹²tê must not be ¹³ts'ên ¹⁴tz'ŭ incongruous and ¹⁵pu-¹⁶ch'i uneven. "The size of the registers must be the same throughout the t'uan (volunteer districts); not of different lengths and breadths." (Wade, 111 & 112; cf. 51 col. 4; 105 col. 8; 278 col. 12; 298 col. 9; 389 col. 9.)

一併 i-ping denotes that the action of the verb is to be attributed "conjointly" to two or more subjects and thus presupposes a plurality of nouns.

今¹ 本² 府³ 酌⁴ 定⁵ 規⁶ 條⁷ 與⁸ 保⁹ 甲¹⁰ 章¹¹ 程¹² 一¹³ 併¹⁴ 飭¹⁵ 匠¹⁶ 刊¹⁷ 刷¹⁸—¹chin now ²pên ³fu I, the prefect ¹⁵ch'ih order ¹⁰chiang the workman to ¹³i-¹⁴ping alike ¹⁷k'an ¹⁸shua cut on boards and print the ⁶kuei ⁷t'iao articles ⁴cho ⁵ting framed (by him) ⁸yü together with the ⁹pao ¹⁰chia registration-system ¹¹chang ¹²ch'êng regulations. "The Prefect has framed certain regulations, which he has ordered the block cutters to print with those affecting the tithing and train-band system." (Wade, 115; for further examples cf. 33 col. 8; 35 col. 8; 36 col. 9; 38 col. 12; 50 col. 5; 59 col. 12; 102 col. 2; 237 col. 9; 248 col. 4.)

凡¹ 在² 番³ 邦⁴ 貿⁵ 易⁶ 寓⁷ 民⁸ 無⁹ 論¹⁰ 例¹¹ 前¹² 例¹³ 後¹⁴ 果¹⁵ 因¹⁶ 貨¹⁷ 帳¹⁸ 未¹⁹ 清²⁰ 不²¹ 能²² 依²³ 限²⁴ 同²⁵ 籍²⁶ 者²⁷ 一²⁸ 概²⁹ 准³⁰ 其³¹ 同³² 籍³³—¹fan ²⁷chê all those who, being ⁷liang good ⁸min people, subjects ⁵mao-⁶yi trading ²tsai in a ³fan foreign ⁴pang kingdom ⁹wu ¹⁰lun no matter whether ¹²ch'ien before ¹¹li (the issue of) the law or ¹⁴hou after ¹³li (the issue of) the law, ¹⁵kuo if really ¹⁶yin because of ¹⁷huo ¹⁸chang goods accounts ¹⁹wei not being ²⁰ch'ing clear, settled ²¹pu ²²nêng they cannot ²³i conformably with ²⁴hsien the limit ²⁵hui ²⁶chi return home, ³¹ch'i they (are) ²⁸i-²⁹kai all, one and all, ³⁰chun allowed ³²hui ³³chi to return home. "Whatsoever persons, being good subjects, have been trading in foreign states, whether they left China before or after the enactment (above cited), provided that their real reason, for not returning within the time allowed, was their inability to close their accounts, have one and all permission to return to their homes." (Wade, 129; cf. 60 col. 2; 81 col. 11; 411 col. 4.)

梁¹ 萬² 和³ 訛⁴ 聞⁵ 蘇⁶ 萬⁷ 全⁸ 弟⁹ 兄¹⁰ 一¹¹ 同¹² 在¹³ 彼¹⁴ ¹*liang* ²*wan* ³*ho* Liang Wan-ho ⁴*ngo* by mistake ⁵*wên* heard, was informed, that ⁶*su* ⁷*wan* ⁸*ch'üan* Su Wan-ch'üan and ⁹*ti*-¹⁰*hsiung* his elder and younger brother were ¹¹*i*-¹²*t'ung* altogether ¹³*tsai*-¹⁴*pi* there. "Liang Wan-'ho had been informed by mistake that he (Su Wan-chüan) was there as well as his elder and younger brother." (Wade, 191; cf. 225 col. 12.)

十¹ 二² 日³ 偕⁴ 抵⁵ 沈⁶ 成⁷ 璧⁸ 家⁹ 一¹⁰ 齊¹¹ 進¹² 內¹³ — ¹*shih*-²*êrh* ³*jih* on the twelfth day ⁴*hsieh* all ⁵*ti* came to ⁹*chia* the house of ⁶*shên* ⁷*ch'ên*-⁸*pi* Shên Ch'ên-pi, and ¹⁰*i*-¹¹*ch'i* all in a body ¹²*chin* entered ¹³*nei* its interior (191).

NUMERAL PHRASES.

(6) Certain numeral phrases express a totality, and hence a plurality of nouns, because only so many individual objects of the denomination represented by the noun are either now, or were at some former time believed to exist (Schott, p. 156), *e.g.* 四海 *ssŭ hai*, the four seas, all the seas, all within the seas, mankind; 四方 *ssŭ fang*, the four regions, all regions, everywhere; 五穀 *wu ku* the five kinds of grain, all kinds of grain, "grain;" 百果 *pai kuo*, the hundred kinds of fruit, all kinds of fruit, "fruit;" 百官 *pai kuan* the Mandarins; 百般 *pai pan*, 千般 *ch'ien pan*, 萬般 *wan pan* all kinds of things, many ways; 萬德 *wan tê* all virtues, or virtues; 萬世 *wan shih* for many ages; 千計 *ch'ien*

chi, a variety of plans ; 百姓 *po hsing* the hundred surnames, the people ; 萬民 *wan min* the ten thousand people, *i.e.* all the people, the masses ; 萬物 *wan wu*, ten thousand things, everything ; 萬國 *wan kuo* the ten thousand nations, all nations ; "international ;" similarly 兆民 *chao min*, "the million." (*See* Part II : "Numerical Categories," in Mayers' *The Chinese Readers' Manual*.)

REDUPLICATION.

(7) Totality may be expressed by reduplication : 人 *jên*, man ; 人人 *jên jên* every man, all men ; 處 *ch'u*, a place ; 處處 *ch'u ch'u* everywhere, at all the places.

等 *têng*.

(8) One of the principal modes of expressing the plural is, in the business style, the addition of the substantive 等 *têng*, class ; also 類 *lei* category, and 輩 *pei*, kind, *e.g.*

該弁等 *kai pien têng*, the said officers (394).

所¹捕² 之³ 人⁴ 等⁵—⁴*jên* ⁵*têng* the men ¹*so* .. ³*chih* who, that ²*pu* were seized (11).

本道等 *pên tao têng* we, the Tao-t'ais (23).

本大臣等 *pên ta ch'ên têng* we, the ministers of state (49).

該洋人等 *kai yang jên têng* the said foreigners (49).

蟻等 *i-têng* "the ants," modest designation of the writers in petitions : "we, the petitioners."

民等 *min-têng* "common men," a modest designation of the writers in petitions : "we, the petitioners."

土匪等 *t'u fei têng* outlaws (103).

該兵勇等 *kai ping yung têng* the said regulars and volunteers (100).

我等 *wo-têng* we.

汝等 *ju-têng*, 爾等 *êrh-têng* you *(plural)*.

爾士民等 *êrh shih min têng* you, the literati and people (110 col. 8).

伊等 *i-têng* they.

該書等 *kai shu têng* the said Shupan *(plural)*, "these clerks" (Wade, 143. col. 10).

原被人等 *yüan pei jên têng*(= 原告被告 etc.), "the complainant and defendant"(Wade, 151 col. 7).

臣等 *ch'ên-têng* the servants, "your Majesty's servants," a respectful designation used by Ministers of State when speaking of themselves in memorials to the throne and such like documents.

該縣等官紳 *kai hsien têng kuan shên*, the magistrates and notables of those districts (169).

農佃人等 *nung tien jên têng*, "small farmers and farm labourers" (Wade, 173).

親等 *ch'in têng*, relatives (185).

該犯等 *kai fan têng*, the said culprits (207).

族隣人等 *ts'u lin jên têng*, kinsmen (215).

某某等 *mou mou têng*, such and such people, "the parties so-and-so" (Wade, 111).

(9) The character 等 *têng* is very frequently added to one or several proper names. If added to the name of one individual it is to be translated *and others*; if it follows the names of more than one individual it simply expresses the plurality of the persons mentioned and should not be translated. The same may be said of names of localities and all other names accompanied by *têng*. 省渡新永秦

等 *shĕng tu hsin yung t'ai tĕng* means "the provincial boat establishment Hsin-yung-t'ai and others," or "the Hsin-yung-t'ai and other establisments" (27col. 1); 舖戶聯德店等 *p'u hu lien tê tien tĕng*, "the Lien Tê and other shops" (27 col. 5). But 呂順陳廣銓萬順泰等 *lü shun ch'ĕn kuang ch'üan wan shun t'ai tĕng* in the same despatch should merely be rendered by the three names: "Lü Shun, Ch'ên Kuang-ch'üan and Wan Shun-t'ai" (27 col. 6).

This, it apears to me, is the rule with regard to 等 *tĕng* when simply following proper names. I am not prepared to say whether it is always strictly adhered to, but should be guided by it whenever it is of importance to know whether an undetermined or a fixed number of individuals is spoken of. It appears, though, that the rule is less certain, if 等 *tĕng* is added to an enumeration of proper names as well as general names in connection with another substantive, following *tĕng*, as 文¹ 武² 等³ 官⁴ ¹*wĕn* civil and ²*wu* military ³*tĕng* ⁴*kuan* officers, which includes only the two kinds of officers enumerated; whereas 洋葯茶葉等貨 *yang-yao ch'a-yeh tĕng huo* "Opium, Tea and the like goods," or "Opium, Tea, etc.," would suggest that other goods besides those enumerated be included. Generally speaking, if the names enumerated be many, 等 *tĕng* loses its generalising force, which is, of course, necessarily retained, if it follows only one name.

安¹ 遠² 公³ 等⁴ 名⁵ 號⁶—¹*an* ²*yüan* ³*kung* An-yüan Kung and ⁴*tĕng* ⁵*ming* ⁶*hao* other designations (214 col. 8); but:

印¹ 汛² 等³ 官⁴—the ¹*yin* holding seal and ²*hsün* executive ³*tĕng* ⁴*kuan* officers (124 col. 12).

二十五六等日—*ĕrh shih wu liu tĕng jih* the 25th and 26th days.

道光八九十一等年 tao kuang pa ch'iu shih i têng nien, the 8th, 9th, and 11th years of Tao-kuang (274).*

類 lei.

(10) 類, or 類 lei, kind, category, may be looked at as a sign of the plural when following certain nouns, as 畜類 ch'u-lei domestic animals; 蟲類 chung-lei, insects; 匪類 fei-lei, robbers, outlaws; 快丁類 k'uai ting lei, the k'uai ting (plural) (162).

輩 pei.

(11) 輩 or 輩 pei, generation, class, kind. 尊輩 tsun pei you, the honoured ones, i.e. those older than the speaker;

* The character 等 têng, which as a substantive frequently occurs in the sense of "class" (頭等 t'ou têng, of the first class; 上等 shang têng, 下等 hsia têng, of the first, second class, etc.,) or "degree" and as a verb means "to wait" (等候 têng hou, to wait), is very often used to pluralise and generalise. Its generalising force clearly appears in connection with the pronoun "this:" 此等 tz'ŭ têng, of this class, i.e. such, talis. Similarly we have to explain certain expressions which, in the business style, quite commonly appear at the end of quotations. When the words used by another writer (or speaker) are quoted, the quotation is closed by adding the words 等語 têng yü, "such words;" similarly, a quotation, or the relation of facts contained in a report, may be closed by adding the words 等因 têng yin, "such arguments," 等由 têng yu, or 等情 têng ch'ing, "such circumstances," "such facts," or 等事 têng shih, "such matters;" if an accusation is the subject of the quotation, 等詞 têng tz'ŭ, "such charges;" after an enumeration of malpractices or nuisances, 等弊 têng pi, "such malpractices," etc., etc. Such concluding phrases need not be translated; they simply show that a quotation or an enumeration of facts, arguments, circumstances, charges, malpractices, etc., is concluded, and correspond to what in English writing would be expressed by inverted commas. If a plurality of arguments is alluded to in the concluding phrase, the character 各 ko, often precedes, e.g. 各等因 ko têng-yin, "all these," or "all such arguments." 等 têng, also retains its generalising force in the phrase 不等 pu têng, after numerals, when the writer does not wish, or is not able, to exactly determine a quantity to be mentioned; translate "or;" "or so," etc. 二三尺至六七尺不等 êrh san ch'ih chih liu ch'i ch'ih pu têng, three or four feet to six or seven feet.

卑 輩 *pei pei*, the opposite of the former as a term of modesty: we, the low ones; *i.e.* your juniors (*cf.* Williams, *Syllabic Dict.*, p. 670); 惡 輩 *o pei* the wicked; 前 輩 *ch'ien pei* predecessors; 後 輩 *hou pei* successors; 忘 義 之 輩 *wang-i chih pei*, the unjust; 夷 輩 *i pei*, barbarians, foreigners; 我 輩 *wo pei*, people of my kind, *i.e.* "we;" 爾 輩 *érh pei*, people of your kind, *i.e.* "you" (plural); 此 輩 *tz'ŭ pei*, these people.

該 *kai* AND 所有 *so yu*.

(12) The terms 該 *kai*, frequently translated by "the said," "the proper," and 所有 *so yu*, usually omitted in translations, very often have a peculiar force somewhat correponding to that of the definite article in ancient Greek or modern European languages. The article, both definite and indefinite, seems at the first glance to be a part of speech which may, without inconvenience, be given up entirely, of which fact the Latin language, one of the most perfect the West has known, is an eloquent proof. Still, where it exists, it is a great linguistic comfort as it were. In Greek as well as in the Teutonic and Romance languages, differences may be expressed by it which it would be either impossible, or very hard to render in a Latin version. In many cases, its exact translation would be immaterial and often spoil the rythm of the language; where it is of importance, however, the indefinite article finds its representative in certain indefinite pronouns, as *quidam, aliquis*, etc., or the numeral *unus*, while the definite article will in most cases be sufficiently, though somewhat too strongly, rendered by some demonstrative pronoun, as *hic, is*, or *ille*, the latter containing the linguistic origin of the article in the Romance languages.

How the necessity for a word like the definite article is felt in modern speech, may be observed by all who listen to the eloquence of some speaker of modern conversational

Latin, who will use more *ille's* in a sentence than Cicero would in a chapter. The same tendency to individualise nouns which has probably led to the gradual formation of the article may be occasionally observed in modern Chinese, both colloquial and written. This tendency, in connection with the entire absence of a word corresponding to our article, explains that over-frequent use made of the demonstrative pronoun 這個 *chei ko* in the Peking, or 呢的 *ni ti* in the Canton colloquial by all speakers who care more for distinctness than elegance.* It would be hard to discover a similar tendency in the ancient written language, and this may account for the entire neglect this question has found at the hands of former grammarians. In the modern business style, however, I venture to observe, there are representatives of what in Greek, Hebrew, and the modern European languages would be expressed by the *definite article.*

This part of speech, in so far as it performs the service of individualizing nouns, *i.e.* of distinguishing one or several individuals from others of the same category or kind, may be said to be employed in two classes of cases.

(13) If an individual or individuals already known or previously mentioned, are to be distinguished from others of the same class not previously known to the reader, the definite article may serve to express the distinction; *e.g.* "Consul A. informed Captain B. that he could not comply with his request; and as *the* Consul had full authority to do so, there remained nothing for *the* Captain, but, etc." Here the definite article *the* in "*the* Consul" and *the* Captain"

---

* Something similar was apparently meant by Gonçalves on p. 129 of his *Arte China*, who under the heading "*O Artigo*," in the grammatical part of this work quotes the example: "a letra *ti* significa terra: 那個地字解說土," translating *na-ko ti-tzŭ* by "*the* letter *ti*."

expresses that "Consul A." and "Captain B." were previously mentioned, and that no other Consuls or Captains are meant. The definite article in such a case will, in the business style, be very frequently found to be expressed by the charater 該 *kai* " to belong to ; proper ; what was spoken of, the aforesaid, the before-mentioned ; that thing, the one, etc." *cf.* Williams, *Syll. Dict.*, p. 306.)

It will, of course, in many cases be found necessary to give this character its full force and translate: "the said," "the proper," "the respective," "this," "that," etc., as circumstances may require; but usually the definite article " *the* " will be found to be sufficient in rendering a word which in some documents occurs in nearly every sentence.

該府 *kai fu*, "the Prefect of the Department."

該守 *kai shou*, "the Prefect."

該縣 *kai hsien*, "the Magistrate."

該地方文武 *kai ti-fang wên wu*, the civil and military (authorities) of the place (220 col. 4).

該省地方官, *kai shêng ti-fang kuan* "the local authorities of the province," or "of that province," viz. Fukien, proviously mentioned (18 col. 3).

該處道臺 *kai ch'u tao-t'ai* "the Tao-t'ai of the place" or "of that place."

巳[1] 飭[2] 該[3] 領[4] 事[5] 官[3]—[2]*ch'ih* ordered [1]*i* (sign of the past: [1]*i*-[2]*chih*) orders had been sent to [3]*kai* the [4]*ling*-[5]*shih*-[6]*kuan* consuls.

該火輪船 *kai huo-lun-ch'uan*, "the steamers" (previously mentioned); "these steamers."

It should be remarked that the character 該 *kai* is, by official etiquette, not allowed to be placed before the titles of superiors. The Emperor may say 該臣 *kai ch'ên* "the Minister," "the said Minister", or 該部 *kai pu*, "the Board," which board is understood to be known by readers, hence "the proper board;" a Prefect may use the word when speaking of a District Magistrate, etc., but not *vice versâ*. *Cf.* Wade's Note 19 to Paper 31.

(41) If an individual or individuals are distinguished from others of the same class by some attribute (adjective, participle, relative clause, etc.) or otherwise, no matter whether or not previously mentioned, the definite article marks the distinction; *e.g.* "*the* circumstances attending the case;" *the* articles of the Treaty;" "*the* buildings that were left behind," etc. The article in such cases is often found to be represented by the phrase 所有 *so-yu*, properly a short relative clause, "the so-and-so that there is," or "that there are," but hardly translatable as such. (Wade: "that which is," "whatsoever there be;" *cf.* Notes No. 23 in Paper 2, *Key* p. 5, and No. 23 in Paper 9, *Key*, p. 12.)

所¹ 有² 劄³ 飭⁴ 管⁵ 理⁶ 口⁷ 岸⁸ 之⁹ 甯¹⁰ 紹¹¹ 台¹² 道¹³ 公¹⁴ 文¹⁵ 一¹⁶ 角¹⁷—¹*so*-²*yu* THE ¹⁴*kung* ¹⁵*wǎn* ¹⁶*i* ¹⁷*chio* despatch (¹⁶*i*-¹⁷*chio*, classifier of "despatches," etc., denoting that there was but "one" despatch) ³*cha*-⁴*ch'ih* ordering, conveying instructions for ¹³*tao* the Tao-t'ai of ¹⁰*ning* ¹*shao* ¹²*t'ai* Ning-po, Shao-Hsing and T'ai-chou ⁹*chih*(relative pronoun): who ⁵*kuan*-⁶*li* manages, is in charge of ⁷*k'ou*-⁸*an* the port. "The letter of instructions he has written to the Intendants of the circuit of Ningpo, Shao-hsing, and T'ai-chou, who is Superintendent of Customs at the port in question" (4).

所¹ 有² 現³ 約⁴ 五⁵ 條⁶—¹*so*-²*yu* the ⁶*wu* five ⁶*t'iao* articles of ³*hsien* the present ⁴*yüeh* treaty.

所¹ 有² 審³ 明⁴ 定⁵ 擬⁶ 緣⁷ 由⁸ ¹*so*-²*yu* the ⁷*yüan-yu* circumstances of ³*shěn*-⁴*ming* investigating and ⁵*ting*-⁶*i* giving judgment. "The conclusions arrived at on investigation, and the sentences awarded" (Wade, 197; 295 col. 2).

所¹ 有² 民³ 間⁴ 田⁵ 地⁶—¹so-²yu the ⁵t'ien-⁶ti field-ground, i.e. cultivated ground ⁴chien at, amongst ³min the people (237).

所¹ 有² 查³ 明⁴ 江⁵ 蘇⁶ 地⁷ 方⁸—¹so-²yu the ⁷ti ⁸fang localities of ⁵chiang ⁶su Kiangsoo ³ch'a ⁴ming examined (238).

所¹ 有² 上³ 元⁴ 等⁵ 六⁶ 縣⁷—¹so-²yu the ⁶liu six ⁷hsien districts ³shang-⁴yüan Shang-yüan ⁵têng, and others; "etc." (258).

所¹ 有² 章³ 程⁴ 列⁵ 後⁶—¹so-²yu the ³chang-⁴ch'êng regulations ⁵lieh are given, ⁶hou hereafter (110; 116 col. 11). The attribute of the noun "regulations" is not mentioned, but to be applied in mind as the context clearly shows that "regulations regarding the train-band system, etc." are meant.

---

(15) The numeral 一 i, one, the equivalent of which is, in certain Western languages, used as the indefinite article a, an, has in Chinese in certain combinations the force of the *definite* article in as much as it individualises a noun as a special thing amongst many of its class, e.g.

至¹ 甬² 商³ 一⁴ 事⁵ ¹chih as to ⁴i the ⁵shih matter, case of ²t'ung-³shang foreign trade, "in the matter of foreign trade," "regarding the subject of foreign trade" (3. col. 8); i here individualises the *shih*, matter, as one out of many matters having been the subject of correspondence previously.

The words 一 桨 i an preceded by a short recapitulation of the details of a case means "in the case of....," "re" (32, col. 9; cf. 34 col. 11; 37 col. 7).

是¹ 以² 臬³ 府⁴ 示⁵ 內⁶ 將⁷ 團⁸ 練⁹ 一¹⁰ 層¹¹ 附¹² 於¹³ 保¹⁴ 甲¹⁵ 章¹⁶ 程¹⁷ 之¹⁸ 內¹⁹ ¹shih-²i therefore ³pei-⁴fu the prefect ⁶nei in ⁵shih his proclamation ¹²fu has inclosed ⁷chiang (sign of the object) ¹⁰i the ¹¹ts'êng scheme of ⁸t'uan-⁹lien train-bands ¹³yü-¹⁸chih ¹⁹nei in ¹⁴pao ¹⁵chia ¹⁶chang ¹⁷ch'êng the regulations respecting the tithing system (106, col. 1; cf. 332, col. 6; 342 col. 2). "The writer has appended the scheme of train-band organization to the regulations affecting the tithing system."

一 事 *i shih* in the matter [of all that precedes in that sentence, *i.e. re* so and so]; see p. 27, col. 2.

冊 後 一 頁 *ts'è-hou i yeh* on the leaf following the list; "the last leaf of the volume" (Wade, 111, col. 9).

君¹ 臣² 一³ 倫⁴ ³*i* the ⁴*lün* relation of, between ¹*chün* sovereign and ²*ch'ên* subject.

THE SUBJECT.

(16) The subject in a sentence is in the first instance distinguished by its position. It is not an arbitrary rule, but the natural run of human thought that makes us think of the subject first; for even in languages where position is by no means material in distinguishing the parts of speech, cases in which the subject stands behind are exceptions from the rule by which the *subject* is placed *before* the *verb* and the *object*.

南¹ 洋² 諸³ 番⁴ 不⁶ 能⁶ 爲⁷ 害⁶ ¹*nan*-²*yang*-³*chu*-⁴*fan* the foreigners of the Southern Sea (subject) ⁵*pu*-⁶*nêng* cannot ⁷*wei* do ⁸*hai* harm (314).

國¹ 家² 征³ 糧⁴ 以⁵ 養⁶ 兵⁷ 朝⁸ 廷⁹ 設¹⁰ 官¹¹ 以¹² 衞¹³ 民¹⁴ —¹*kuo*-²*chia* the government (subject) ³*chêng* collects (verb) ⁴*liang* land taxes (object) ⁵*i* in order to ⁶*yang* feed ⁷*ping* the soldier; ⁸*ch'ao*-⁹*t'ing* the court (subject) ¹⁰*shè* establishes, appoints (verb) ¹¹*kuan* mandarins (object) ¹²*i* in order to ¹³*wei* protect ¹⁴*min* the people (443).

本¹ 大² 臣³ 自³ 當⁵ 如⁶ 期⁷ 前⁸ 往⁹ 該¹⁰ 處¹¹—¹*pên* I; the ²*ta*-³*ch'ên* minister of state (subject) ⁴*tzŭ* of course ⁵*tang* must ⁸*ch'ien*-⁹*wang* proceed to ¹⁰*kai*-¹¹*ch'u* the place (previously mentioned) ^6ju according to, by $^7ch'i$ the appointed time. "It will be, of course, the Commissioner's duty to be at the place, named at the time specified" (15).

(17) In Chinese exceptions are only allowed when common sense excludes all misconstruction, as if we were to say in English "*a cake the boy eats,*" instead of "*the boy eats a cake.*" The object is sometimes placed before the subject at the head of the sentence, for the sake of emphasis. In a certain class of Imperial edicts for instance, specimens of which are very frequent in the *Peking Gazette*, examples of the following kind are of stereotyped occurrence:—

原¹ 告² 吳³ 超⁴ 宗⁵ 該⁶ 部⁷ 照⁸ 例⁹ 解¹⁰ 往¹¹ 俻¹² 質¹³—
("I, the Emperor, command that," or "Let," 著 *cho*, to be supplied from the preceding): Let ^6kai ^7pu the proper board (subject) $^{10}chieh$-$^{11}wang$ ^{12}pei-$^{13}chih$ forward for confrontation (verb) ^1yüan-^2kao ^3wu-$^4ch'ao$-^5tsung, the plaintiff Wu Ch'ao-tsung (object) ^8chao-^9li according to law. "Let the proper Board, as the law requires, send the plaintiff forward to be confronted [with the accused]" (134; *cf.* 150 col. 11; 175 col. 8).

(18) If the same object belongs to different verbs with different subjects, as if we would say in English "heroes enjoy, cowards fear, the beat of the war drum," this kind of inversion is frequently resorted to in Chinese; the object, then, appears at the head of the sentence, but the verb is followed by 之 *chih*, "illud" "it," resuming it as it were at the proper place, *e.g.*

此¹ 種² 兇³ 徒⁴ 不⁵ 但⁶ 州⁷ 縣⁸ 疾⁹ 之¹⁰ 如¹¹ 仇¹² 吏¹³ 胥¹⁴ 尤¹⁵ 畏¹⁶ 之¹⁷ 如¹⁸ 虎¹⁹ ^3hsiung-$^4t'u$ villains of $tz'ŭ$ this ^2chung class, *i.e.* this class of villains ^5pu not ^6tan only ^7chou the Chou Magistrates and ^8hsien the Hsien Magistrates ^9chi hate $^{10}chih$ them ^{11}ju like $^{12}ch'ou$ enemies, ^{13}li-$^{14}hsü$ the clerks and writers ^{15}yu still more ^{16}wei fear $^{17}chih$ them ^{18}ju

like [19] *hu* tigers; "not only do the magistrates hate this kind of villains like enemies, but the yamên writers even fear them like tigers" (265).

(19) Where the subject is clearly mentioned as in the above examples it is easy enough to recognise it. This is, however, not always the case. The subject is very frequently either to be supplied from the preceding or the general context, or the verb is an impersonal one, as "it is necessary to, etc.;" "*one* must;" "*one* has, will, does, etc.," thus leaving it entirely to the imagination of the reader who the doer of the action described may be. It is but natural that, with regard to this point, any attempt to find grammatical rules by way of analogy should prove a failure; common sense and close attention to the logical run of the general context is the only recommendable guide. The same subject is often to be applied to several verbs, objects, etc., and may be the only one to be discovered in whole strings of sentences; and here it should be noted that the Chinese are not over particular with regard to the logical connexion between the subject and its verb, just as we occasionally say in English "tea pays an Export Duty of two taels five candareens," without considering that it is not the tea, but the merchant who pays the duty on it. Now this kind of anomaly is carried to the extreme in the business style. "A junk, laden with stones, crosses the sea, is seized by a cruizer, brought before the Magistrate, squeezed money, not yet released, applies for investigation and release of the men seized." The subject in this case is partly the junk, partly its owner, who writes a petition regarding his ship.

由 *yu,* INTRODUCING THE LOGICAL SUBJECT.

(20) As peculiar to the business style I have to mention here the expression of the "doer of an action," not to say "sub-

ject of a sentence," by the preposition 由 *yu, alias* "from, by way of," if the subject is not inanimate, but a person. The literal explanation of the preposition *yu* in such cases is that it represents the Latin preposition *a* or *ab*, and the noun following it should be made to correspond to a noun in the ablative case in Latin; the verb should be explained as in the passive voice, and the object following it should, strictly speaking, be the nominative. If, in English, instead of "the Governor addresses the Consul," we were to say "by the Governor is addressed the Consul" (由本部院照會領事官 *yu pĕn-pu-yüan chao-hui ling-shih-kuan*), "the Consul" would, in the second example, become the grammatical subject; but the doer of the action expressed by the verb, the *logical* subject, as it were, would always be "the Governor."

Instances in which the literal meaning of 由 (*i.e. a* or *ab, cum ablativo*) may be retained in such sentences without inconvenience in translating are frequent enough (*cf.* 148 col. 4; 149 col. 3); but as a practical rule, I would recommend to simply look at 由 *yu* as a sign of the subject, placed before nouns representing persons.

由[1] 縣[2] 約[3] 束[4] 工[5] 書[6]—[1]*yu* [2]*hsien* the District Magistrate (will) [3]*yüeh-*[4]*shu* restrain, keep in order [5]*kung-*[6]*shu* the clerks of the Works Department (29).

由[1] 縣[2] 發[3] 給[4] 腰[5] 牌[6] 護[7] 照[8]—[1]*yu-*[2]*hsien* the District Magistrate [3]*fa-*[4]*chi* issues [5]*yao-*[6]*p'ai* belt-tickets and [7]*hu-*[8]*chao* passports. Wade:—"A belt-ticket and passport will then be issued to him by the District Magistrate" (103).

由[1] 臬[2] 司[3] 林[4] 則[5] 徐[6] 覆[7] 審[8]—[1]*yu-*[2]*nieh-*[3]*ssŭ* [4]*lin* [5]*ts'-*[6]*hsü* the Commissioner of Justice Lin Tsê-hsü [7]*fu* again [8]*shĕn* tried the case.

由[2] 府[2] 審[3] 明[4]—[1]*yu* [2]*fu* the Prefect of the Department [3]*shĕn-*[4]*ming* tried the case (223).

先¹ 由² 委³ 員⁴ 申⁵ 報⁶ 司⁷ 道⁸—²yu ³wei-yüan the Deputy (must) ¹hsien first ⁵shên-⁶pao report to ⁷ssŭ the high provincial authorities and ⁹tao the Tao-t'ais (268).

由¹ 雲² 南³ 督⁴ 撫⁵ 用⁶ 文⁷ 照⁸ 會⁹ 該¹⁰ 國¹¹ 王¹²—¹yu ⁴tu the Governor General and ⁵fu the Governor of ²yün-³nan Yünnan ⁶yung using ⁷wên characters ⁸chao-⁹hui (should) address in a despatch ¹²wang the king of ¹⁰kai ¹¹kuo the country (previously mentioned). "The Governor General and Governor of Yünnan will address the king in writing" (g76.)

由¹ 該² 處³ 紳⁴ 耆⁵ 聯⁶ 名⁷ 稟⁸ 明⁹— ¹yu ⁴chin-⁵ch'i the gentry of ²kai ³ch'u the place (previously mentioned) will ⁶lien ⁷ming subscribing names ⁸ping-⁹ming petition, i.e., will sign a petition (448).

巳¹ 由² 本³ 關⁴ 部⁵ 另⁶ 造⁷ 純⁸ 銅⁹ 砝¹⁰ 碼¹¹ 備¹² 用¹³— ²yu-³pên-⁴kuan-⁵pu I, the Superintendent of Customs ¹i (sign of the past) have ⁶ling separately, besides, ⁷ts'ao made ⁸ch'un-⁹t'ung solid copper ¹⁰fa-¹¹ma weights ¹²pei-¹³yung to be ready for use (7; cf. Wade's note No. 13, in Paper 4, where 由 yu is explained as "through the instrumentality, by order of;" also "it has been left to me, as my duty").

Further examples:—224 col. 1; 249 col. 10; 257 col. 9; 269 col. 1; 296 col. 7.

(21) When the object in such sentences is expressed by 將 chiang, which is very often the case, though but few examples may be found for it in Wade's collection, we are, it appears, almost forced by the whole construction to look at 由 yu as a sign of the subject, at least from our practical European point of view. For, though we are quite at liberty to construe sentences in whatever way we choose, as long as the true meaning is left uninjured, it must not be forgotten that even 將 chiang, when introducing the object, is only a verb, and that e.g. 由¹ 府² 將³ 犯⁴ 罰⁵ 罪⁶ is with

equal, or better, right rendered: "⁴*fan* the criminal ³*chiang* being taken ¹*yu* by ²*fu* the Prefect ⁵*fa*-⁶*tsui* is punished" than "⁰*yu* ²*fu* the Prefect (subject) ⁵*fa*-⁶*tsui* punishes ³*chiang* ⁴*fan* the criminal (object)." But since 將 *chiang* is by all foreign grammarians practically accepted as a sign of the object or accusative, I cannot help explaining 由 *yu* as a sign of the subject, with this restriction, however, that its original meaning, *a* or *ab cum ablativo*, may occasionally claim its right.

由¹ 各² 該³ 道⁴ 將⁵ 犯⁶ 發⁷ 回⁸—¹*yu* (marking the subject) ³*kai* the proper, the respective ²*ko* ⁴*tao* Tao-tais ⁷*fa* ⁸*hui* sent back ⁵*chiang* ⁶*fan* the criminals (object) (147).

THE OBJECT.

(22) The object may be expressed either by position, or by the use of auxiliary characters.

Wherever it is expressed by position *only*, the rule is that it should follow the verb, while the subject is to precede the verb. (*Cf*. Julien, *Syntaxe Nouvelle*, Vol I, p. 16.)

准¹ 照² 會³—¹*chun* to receive (verb) ²*chao*-³*hui* a despatch (object).

照¹ 會² 領³ 事⁴ 官⁵—¹*chao*-²*hui* to address in a despatch (verb) ³*ling*-⁴*shih*-⁵*kuan* the Consul (object).

In the above two examples it is the relative position of the word *chao-hui* that makes it appear as a substantive ("a despatch") or a verb ("to address in a despatch") respectively.

國¹ 家² 養³ 兵⁴—¹*kuo* ²*chia* the Government (subject) ³*yang* feeds (verb) ⁴*ping* soldiers (object).

(23) If, after a verb meaning "to give to," "to tell, to communicate to," "to promise to," etc., a substantive is to be added as corresponding to a noun in the *dative* case, the ³ruling position is as follows:

1. *Subject*. 2 *Verb*. 3 *Dative*. 4 *Object*. (*Cf*. Julien, p. 14).

國¹ 家² 積³ 給⁴ 水⁵ 勇⁶ 口⁷ 粮⁸ 銀⁹ 兩¹⁰—¹kuo-²chia the Government (subject) ³hsü ⁴chi continuously gives (verb) ⁵shui-⁶yung the marine soldiers (dative) ⁷k'ou-⁸liang provisions and ⁹yin-¹⁰liang money (object).

(24) Examples of this kind are, however, so rare and the rule suffers so many exceptions in the business style, that common sense must again be resorted to as the safest guide. For, cases not complying with the rule are frequent enough, especially where misconstruction is excluded by the nature of matters, e.g.

給¹ 文² 羅³ 伯⁴ 聘⁵—¹chi to give (verb) ²wên a letter (object) to ³lo-⁴po-⁵tan Robert Thom (dative) (4); we may here consider the two terms chi, to give, and wên, letter, as having grown together and representing one verb, having "lo-po-tan" as its object, as if we were to say: "to letter-give Robert Thom."

(25) The object is frequenty placed at the head of the sentence for the sake of emphasis as I have shown above.

該¹ 銀² 多³ 少⁴ 希⁵ 示⁶ 知⁷ 以⁸ 便⁹ 如¹⁰ 數¹¹ 付¹² 還¹³—⁵hsi please ⁶shih ⁷chih make known, let me know (verb) of ¹kai the ²yin money ³to-⁴shao the quantity, i.e. the amount of money due (object) ⁸i-⁹pien in order that ¹⁰ju ¹¹shu as per amount ¹²fu ¹³huan (it may be) refunded (402).

將 chiang, A SIGN OF THE OBJECT.

(26) Of auxiliary characters serving to mark the object 將 chiang, "to take," is the most prominent.* It corresponds exactly to 把 pa ("to take" and sign of the object) of the Mandarin colloquial. (See Bazin, Grammaire mandarine, p. 67, and Edkins, Mandarin Grammar, p. 122).

* 將 chiang was a common sign of the object in the colloquial of the Yüan Dynasty, as may be observed in numerous examples in "L' Orphelin de la Chine," a tragedy written in that style and translated by Julien Syntaxe Nouvelle, pp. 309-406).

The object introduced by 將 *chiang* always precedes the verb, but follows the subject. If the noun to be placed in the *accusative* by this auxiliary character is accompanied by attributes (genitive, adjective, relative clause, etc.) such attributes are placed between 將 *chiang* and the noun to which they belong.

該¹ 船² 必³ 須⁴ 將⁵ 茶⁶ 葉⁷ 裝⁸ 回⁹ 香¹⁰ 港¹¹—¹*kai* the (previously mentioned) ²*ch'uan* ship ³*pi*-⁴*hsü* must, ⁸*chuang* loading ⁵*chiang* ⁶*ch'a*-⁷*yeh* the tea (object) ⁹*hui* return to ¹⁰*hsiang*-¹¹*chiang* Hongkong (17).

將¹ 車² 輛³ 折⁴ 回⁵—⁴*chè* ⁵*hui* they turned back ¹*chiang*-²*ch'ê*-³*liang* (their) carts (object) (49).

現¹ 將² 執³ 照⁴ 帶⁵ 回⁶ 本⁷ 衙⁸ 門⁹—(subject: "they," to be supplied) ¹*hsien* now ⁵*tai* ⁶*hui* bring back to ⁷*pên*-⁸*ya*-⁹*mên* my, the writer's, Yamên ²*chiang* ³*chi*-⁴*chao* the passports (object) (49). The above is one of the very numerous examples in which we in vain look for a subject of the sentence; in such cases the passive will often be resorted to with advantage as in Wade's translation: "These passports were brought back to this Yamên."

將¹ 被² 拿³ 之⁴ 人⁵ 立⁶ 即⁷ 釋⁸ 放⁹ 矣¹⁰—to ⁶*li*-⁷*chi* at once ⁸*shih*-⁹*fang* release ¹*chiang*-⁵*jên* the men (object) ⁴*chih* (relative particle) who ²*pei* (sign of the passive) were, had been ³*na* seized ¹⁰*i* final particle, untranslateable; corresponding to a period (11). The relative ²*pei* ³*na* ⁴*chih*, "who had been seized," being an attribute of ⁵*jên*, is placed between that word and ¹*chiang*, the sign of the object.

(27) The object with the auxiliary character 將 *chiang* placed *before* the verb allows of another object being added *after* the verb in such cases where e.g. in Latin we use a double accusative, *i.e.* chiefly in connexion with verbs meaning "to declare as, to consider as," etc.

將¹ 高² 地³ 捏⁴ 報⁵ 低⁶ 窪⁷—¹*chiang* (sign of the object)

^2kao altum ^3ti solum ^4nieh falso ^5pao declarare ^6ti-^7wa humilem sc. solum ; " to fraudulently return high land as low " (135).

---

(28) It has been remarked that 把 *pa*, "to take" as a sign of the object is peculiar to the colloquial language. This does not, however, preclude its occurring in documents as a colloquial word, especially in the minutes of all kinds of enquiries when the very words used by a witness are given in his deposition, *e.g.*

求¹ 把² 我³ 交⁴ 本⁵ 國⁶ 在⁷ 省⁸ 英⁹ 商¹⁰ 收¹¹ 領¹²—^1chiu I beg ^4chiao to hand ^2pa-^3wo me $^{11}shou$ $^{12}ling$ over to ^9ying the British $^{10}shang$ merchants ^5pĕn-^6kuo of my country ^7tsai in ^8shĕng the province, or provincial capital. "I beg that I may be given into the hands of some English merchant residing at Canton" (6).

以 *i*, INTRODUCING THE OBJECT.

(29) The particle next in importance to 將 *chiang* as a mark of the object is 以 *i*, "to use." It has ever been the pride of the late Professor Julien to have discovered, as it were, the power possessed by this word of marking the accusative, and the result of his researches may be found laid down on pp. 15 and 20—27 of his *Syntaxe Nouvelle* (Vol. I). While referring the student to his notes on the accusative as a chapter that may be read with especial advantage, I must state with regard to 以 *i*, that in the modern documentary style, its use as a sign of the object is not only more restricted but also somewhat different from that described by Julien. In the *Ku-wĕn* 以 *i* is used in the same manner as 將 *chiang* in the modern style, *i.e.* it introduces an object and with it, precedes the verb.

以¹ 天² 下³ 與⁴ 人⁵—¹i um ²t'ien-³hsia imperi-(imperium) ⁴yü dare ⁵jên hominibus. (Julien, l.c., p. 23.) "To give the empire to man."*

This, it appears, is the rule in the classical style, while examples where 以 i with the object *follow* the verb are exceptional, as the following:

分¹ 人² 以³ 財⁴—¹fên distribuere ²jên hominibus ³i as ¹ts'ai diviti-(divitias). (Julien, p. 24.) "To ¹fên distribute, give ²jên the men, people ³i ⁴ts'ai riches."

In the business style, however, cases where the object, introduced by 以 i, *follows* the verb, are quite as frequent as the opposite construction is exceptional.

(30) The classical use is always retained in that very common phrase which is formed by the verb 爲 wei "to make, to consider as," preceded by an accusative with 以 i. Just as the verb 報 pao in the example quoted above (paragraph 27: "*altum solum declarare humilem*") the verb 爲 wei in this case has a two-fold object, and is thus comparable to the Latin phrases *facere aliquem aliquid; nominare, estimare*, etc., *aliquem aliquid; viz.*: 1. the immediate object (*aliquem*) and 2. the supplementary object (*aliquid*). In the Chinese phrase i....wei...., the immediate object, introduced by i always precedes the verb wei, while the supplementary object follows it as an accusative by position.

以¹ 妻² 爲³ 妾⁴—¹i ²ch'i uxorem ³wei facere ⁴ch'ieh pellicem (object by position). "To treat a wife as a concubine" (187).

無¹ 不² 以³ 彈⁴ 壓⁵ 地⁶ 方⁷ 爲⁸ 屬⁹—The immediate object is, in this example, represented by a complete sentence, ⁴t'an-⁵ya-⁶ti-⁷fang, "to keep the country in order," or "the

* Julien's translation says "imperium donare hominibus;" this may be expressed in Latin by "imperio donare homines," without altering the sense. This latter form may serve as a key to the Chinese construction.

keeping in order of the country," which in Greek would be preceded by the neutral article τό.

¹*Wu* ²*pu* not (that he does) not, *i.e.* he always does ⁸*wei* make ³*i* (sign of the object) ⁴*t'an*-⁵*ya* ⁶*ti*-⁷*fang* the keeping in order of the country ⁹*chu* an enjoinment (supplementary object, accusative by position). "He never fails to enjoin them (*viz.*, the local authorities) to maintain order" (18).

以¹ 遠² 年³ 墳⁵ 碑⁶ 記⁷ 爲⁸ 憑⁹—²*yüan* remoti ³*nien* anni ¹*i* (sign of the object) ⁴*fên*-⁵*mu* sepulcralem ⁶*pei*-⁷*chi* inscriptionem ⁸*wei* facere ⁹*p'ing* argumentum; to claim land "on the ground of an old grave stone inscription."

以 *i* and 爲 *wei* have in the sense of "to consider as," etc., grown so much together that the two words joined are used as a compound verb having the same sense.

曾¹ 經² 發³ 奧⁴ 執⁵ 照⁶ 在⁷ 民⁸ 等⁹ 以¹⁰ 爲¹¹ 永¹² 遠¹³ 基¹⁴ 業¹⁵—⁵*chi*-⁶*chao* deeds ¹*tsĕng*-²*ching* (signs of the past) having been ³*fa*-⁴*yü* issued, ⁷*tsai* at, with, ⁸*min*-⁹*têng* the petitioners ¹⁰*i*-¹¹*wei* were considered ¹²*yung*-¹³*yüan* perpetual ¹⁴*chi*-¹⁵*yeh* proprietorships. "Deeds were issued which on the part of your Petitioners were regarded as assuring them proprietorship in perpetuity" (57).

(31) A construction similar to that formed by 以 *i* and 爲 *wei* is formed by 以 *i* and other verbs meaning to declare, etc.

以¹ 多² 報³ 少⁴—³*pao* to delare ¹*i* ²*to* much (object) as ⁴*shao* little (supplementary object), *i.e.* to understate the quantity of an article.

以¹ 貴² 報³ 賤⁴—³*pao* to declare ¹*i*-²*kuei* dear ⁴*chien* as cheap, *i.e.* to understate the value of an article.

(32) This phrase 以 *i*.. 爲 *wei*.., "to consider," etc., common though it is, appears to be one amongst very few instances of 以 *i* introducing the object *before* the verb, whereas cases in which the object, being expressed by *i*,

comes *after* the verb are frequent enough, more especially after the following classes of verbs:

1. Verbs conveying the sense of a communication, verbal or written, as "to tell, to report, to state, to write, to wish, to express hope, to promise, etc." The object, which appears either as an ordinary noun, or still more frequently in the shape of a complete sentence, is after such verbs introduced by 以 *i*. Where the object is a sentence, this particle may be translated by "that, to the effect that," or be looked at as simply representing what we express by inverted commas, *i.e.* marking a quotation. This use of 以 *i* has become so common in the course of time that even nouns having the sense of such verbs may be followed by it, as "a letter to the effect that," which may be expressed by 函以 *han-i*, etc.

須[1]告[2]以[3]經[4]過[5]之[6]處[7]務[8]將[9]執[10]照[11]呈[12]驗[13]不[14]得[15]故[16]意[17]藏[18]匿[19]不[20]交[21]以[22]符[23]條[24]約[25]—(When in future passports are issued to somebody) [1]*hsü* it is necessary [2]*kao* to say [3]*i* placing all that follows into the accusative case dependent upon [2]*kao*; translate: "that" [7]*ch'u* on the places [6]*chih* (sign of the genitive, here having the power of a relative pronoun) of [4]*ching* [5]*kuo* passing by ([4] [5] [6] [7]=at the places through which he passes) [8]*wu* he must [12]*ch'êng* [13]*yen* deliver for examination [9]*chiang* (sign of the accusative) [10]*chi-*[11]*chao* the passport, and [14]*pu-*[15]*tê* must not [16]*ku-*[17]*i* intentionally [18]*ts'ang-*[19]*ni* conceal and [20]*pu* [21]*chiao* not deliver up, [22]*i* in order to [23]*fu* be in accordance with [24]*t'iao-*[25]*yüeh* the Treaty. "You must inform (the applicant for a passport) that, in conformity with the treaty, he must produce his passport at the places through which he passes, and that he is not to keep it back" (50; cf. 20 col. 10; 190 col 7; 134 col. 1; 269 col. 8: "a proclamation to the effect that, etc.").

欲[1]以[2]個[3]爾[4]寫[5]兒[6]火[7]輪[8]船[9]往[10]來[11]裝[12]貨[13]—

$^1y\ddot{u}$ he wished ^2i converting all that follows into the object of $^1y\ddot{u}$, to wish; translate: "that" ^7huo-^8lun-$^9ch'uan$ the steamer ^3ko-$^4\hat{e}rh$-^5hsieh-$^6\hat{e}rh$ "Corsair" $^{10}wang$-^{11}lai went to and fro, and $^{12}chuang$ carried ^{13}huo merchandise (16; cf. Wade's note to this example; also 25 col. 12).

2. In the case of verbs meaning "to teach" and "to examine" the matter taught and the object of the examination may follow the verb with 以 i.

教¹ 以² 漢³ 書⁴—^1chiao to teach ^2i (sign of the accusative) ^3han Chinese ^4shu books, literature.

教¹ 以² 清³ 書⁴—^1chiao to teach ^2i-$^3ch'ing$-^4shu Manchu literature. (Yungch'êng's Edict of 3rd year, 6th moon, 乙亥 day.)

試¹ 以² 文³ 義⁴—^1shih to examine ^2i (sign of the accusative, introducing the object of the examination) " in " $^3w\hat{e}n$-^4i the explanation of the text (207).

3. After the verbs meaning to accuse, to be guilty of, etc., the crime, which may be looked at as the object of the verb, may follow the verb *with* or *without* 以 i.

坐¹ 以² 罰³—^1tso to be guilty of ^2i (denoting object of ^1tso) ^3fa punishment (348).

4. The verb 加 *chia*, "to add," in its original sense as well as when it means "to inflict" (as a punishment) is frequently followed by 以 i to denote the object. In like manner all verbs meaning "to inflict," "to punish by," "to condemn to" may be followed by an accusative *with*, or *without* 以 i.

加¹ 以² 洪³ 湖⁴ 異⁵ 漲⁶—^1chia add ^2i that, or the fact that [accedit quod] ^3hung-^4hu the Hung Lake ^6chang is overflowing ^5i in an extraordinary manner. "In addition to this, besides, Lake Hung has risen to an unusual height"(230).

加¹ 以² 嚴³ 防⁴—^1chia to add ^2i-^3yen-^4fang strict watch, i.e. to be on one's guard (98).

加¹ 以² 刑³ 嚇⁴—¹chia to inflict, apply ²i (marking the object of ¹chia) ³hsing ⁴ho torture (214).

擬¹ 以² 枷³ 杖⁴—¹i to sentence to ²i (marking the object of ¹i) ³chia the cangue and ⁴chang flogging with the larger bamboo (141; cf. 135 col. 3).

應¹ 擬² 以³ 重⁴ 杖⁵ 發⁶ 落⁷—¹ying it is necessary to ²i award punishment of ³i ⁴chung ⁵chang the heavy bamboo and ⁶fa-⁷lo release (the offender after punishment). "He too should be sentenced to be beaten with the heavier bamboo; after which he will be discharged" (143).

The number of verbs, or of classes of verbs, allowing of a construction similar to the above could be easily increased by collecting a greater number of examples of the kind.

惟 wei.... 是 shih....

(33)   Julien, on page 28 of his *Syntaxe Nouvelle* (Vol. I) comments upon the word 是 shih as a sign of the accusative. He says: "Ce signe qui signifie ordinairement: *esse, rectum, verum, iste, hic, ita est*, m'a paru, dans certains cas, être une sorte de marque d'accusatif, ou plutôt comme un signe qui, placé avant un verbe final, nous autorise à regarder le mot ou les mots qui le précèdent comme régimes de ce verbe."

A similar construction may also be found in the business style, but the examples I have met with all have the restritive 惟 wei, "only," before the object.

惟¹ 中² 人³ 杜⁴ 二⁵ 是⁶ 問⁷—⁷wên to ask, to hold responsible, ¹wei ⁶shih (denoting the object) ²chung ³jên, the middle-man, gobetween ⁴tu-⁵êrh Tu Êrh (84 col. 5; cf. 85 col. 6; 80 col. 4; 76 col. 6).

民¹ 等² 自³ 當⁴ 惟⁵ 命⁶ 是⁷ 聽⁸—¹min-²têng the men of the people, *i.e.* we, the petitioners (subject) ³tzŭ of course ⁴tang have to, are bound to ⁸t'ing obey ⁵wei-⁷shih (denoting the object) ⁶ming orders (object) (58; cf. *Shihking* ii 5.1.4: 惟爾言是聽 "They only hearken to shallow words," Legge).

惟¹ 利⁹ 是³ 嗜⁴—⁴shih to relish ¹wei ³shih (denoting the object) ²li gain (object). "He was [only] desirous of gain."

It appears that, in this class of examples, *wei* and *shih* enclose the term which has to be considered as the object of the verb following *shih*. Cf. *Shuking* ii 5, 1. 4; ii 4. 5. 9; ii 4. 10. 5, quoted in the special treatise on the subject: *Die Partikel* 惟 *wei in Schu-king und Schi-king*, by Dr. Max Uhle. Leipzig, 1880.

The Genitive.

Anteposition. 之 *chih.*

(34) Like the classical style, the business language has two modes of expressing the genitive case, *viz.*. 1. position (anteposition), and 2. the use of the auxiliary character 之 *chih.*

The rule of position is that the noun to be placed in the genitive immediately precedes the term of which it is dependent. I shall in the course of these notes, call this anteposition.*

---

* Anteposition does not serve exclusively to form the genitive, and seeing two nouns placed one before the other, it requires some practice to recognise whether the first be in the possessive case or not. If different nouns (*i.e.* expressions chiefly used as such, whether monosyllabic or polysyllabic) are placed one before the other, the following may be their mutual relation (*cf.* Schott, *Chines. Sprachlehre*, p. 54):

(*a*) They may represent a compound term, each having the same or a similar meaning as the whole expression taken together, *e.g.* 眼 目 *yen.mu*, eye; 朋 友 *p'êng-yu*, friend.

(*b*) They may represent separate terms and have to be connected by *and*, *e.g.* 督 撫²—¹*tu* the Governor General, *and* ²*fu* the Governor 屋¹ 宇² 田³ 園⁴—¹*wu-*²*yü* houses *and* ³*t'ien-*⁴*yüan* land (63 col. 4). In certain cases such nouns may also have to be connected by *or*, as in 兄 弟 *hsiung-ti* the elder *or* younger brother, or brothers.

(*c*) The first may be used as an adjective in so far as it makes the quality described by it attributable to the following noun, *e.g.* 輪 船 *lun-ch'uan*, a wheel-ship, a steamer; 官 名 *kuan-ming*, official style (3 col. 6); 洋 商 *yang-shang*, an ocean merchant, *i.e.* a foreign merchant (6 col. 2).

(*d*) They may be in the relation of subject and predicate, the former always preceding in such a case, as in 民 安 *man, in* the people are quiet, or at peace.

DOCUMENTARY STYLE.   49

(35)   Examples of genitives expressed by antoposition.

天¹ 命²—²ming the decree of ¹t'ien heaven (84).

貴¹ 國² 巡³ 船⁴—³hsün-⁴ch'uan the cruizers of ¹kuei-²kuo your country (59).

各¹ 關² 監³ 督⁴—³chien-⁴tu the Superintendents of ¹ko-²kuan all Custom houses (296).

貴¹ 大² 臣³ 照⁴ 會⁵—⁴chao-⁵hui the despatch of ¹kuei-²ta-³ch'ên your Excellency (4).

本¹ 月² 初³ 旬⁴—³ch'u the first ⁴hsün decade of ¹pên this ²yüeh month (10).

It should be noted that three or more nouns placed one before the other may be dependent upon the following noun, or nouns, as genitives, e.g.

江¹ 蘇² 省³ 各⁴ 州⁵ 廳¹ 縣⁷ 境⁸ 內⁹—⁹nei in the inside of, within ⁸ching the boundaries of ⁴ko ⁵chou ⁶t'ing ⁷hsien the Chou, T'ing and Hsien districts of ³shéng the province of ¹chiang-²su Kiangsu (240).

(36)   The second way of expressing the genitive is the affixing to a noun of the auxiliary character 之 chih which, in the written language, very nearly corresponds to 的 ti in the Mandarin Colloquial and 嘅 ké in the Canton Dialect, e.g.

徐¹ 保² 之³ 屋⁴ 宇⁵ 田⁶ 園⁷—⁴wu-⁵yü the houses and ⁶t'ien-yüan land ³chih of ¹hsü-²pao Hsü Pao (63).

(e) The second noun may be in apposition to the first, e.g. 周 字 chou-tzŭ, the word "chou" (206 col. 9); 樟林地方 chang-lin-ti-fang, the place Chang-lin (5 col. 9).; 全¹ 權² 字³ 樣⁴—³tzŭ-⁴yang the expression ¹ch'üan-²ch'üan "full powers" (3 col. 4).
  If we look at such examples from the point of view of French grammar, we may easily unite this head with the following by translating e.g. the last mentioned example by "l'expression de plein pouvoir."
(f) The first may be a genitive dependent upon the second. To distinguish whether in any particular case anteposition denotes the genitive or any of the other possibilities, common sense on the one hand, and the fixed usage of the language on the other, are the only guides. Common sense would, for instance, forbid our rendering the two characters 督 撫 tu-fu by "the Governor of the Governor General;" but it is the usage exclusively which tells us that 父 母 fu-mu does not mean "the mother of the father," but "father and mother."

年¹ 歲² 之³ 豐⁴ 歉⁵—the ⁴fêng-⁵chien abundance or scarcity, i.e. the prosperity ³chih of ¹nien-²sui a year (116).

Both nouns, the one placed in the genitive as well as the independent one, may, of course, be accompanied by adjectives.

好¹ 心² 之³ 德⁴—⁴té the virtue ³chih of ¹hao ²hsin a good heart (414).

今¹ 日² 之³ 急⁴ 務⁵—⁴chi ⁵wu urgent business ³chih of ¹chin ²jih the present day. "The most pressing necessities of the time" (104 col. 9).

(37) 之 chih as a sign of the genitive may, or may not, be omitted, i.e. anteposition may, or may not, be used instead of the auxiliary character, without altering the sense. But if several genitives are made dependent upon each other, it is the rule that only the last be expressed by 之 chih, while all the preceding ones must be genitives by position. If a preposition precedes the noun, the genitive dependent upon the same is placed between the preposition and its noun, e.g.

於¹ 黑² 夜³ 中⁴—¹yü ⁴chung in the middle of, in ²hei ³yeh the dark night (286; cf. 288 col. 9).

於¹ 進² 口³ 之⁴ 時⁵—¹yü at ⁵shih the time ⁴chih of ²chin ³k'ou entering port (248 col. 2; cf. col. 11).

(38) Certain words corresponding to our prepositions, but which, as they are placed after the noun, should rather be called post-positions, may be said to govern the genitive, both by position and with 之 chih. These words may be looked upon as ablatives (locatives, etc.) of nouns expressing local, temporal, or other relations, such as 中 chung the middle, the inside, ablative: " in the inside;" if a genitive precedes, it receives the meaning " within, in, amongst," as 水¹ 中² ²chung in the inside of ¹shui the water, i.e. " in the water." 內 nei the inside, within, in; 外 wai, the outside,

outside, besides; 間 *chien*, in the place of, at; a time, at the time of, at, in; 後 *hou*, the after time, the after place, after, behind; 前 *ch'ien*, the former time, the place before, before; 上 *shang*, that which is above, above; 下 *hsia*, that which is below, below; perhaps even 以 *i*, "use," in the expressions 是 以 *i* by the use of, *shih*, this, *i.e.* through this, by this, thereby, therefore, and 何 以—*i* by the use of *ho* what, by what, whereby, wherefore.

身¹ 家² 內³—³*nei* in the inside ²*chia* of the house ¹*shên* of myself, *i.e.* in my house (here: "to my house," 72 col. 6).

順¹ 治² 門³ 內⁴ 石⁵ 附⁶ 馬⁷ 大⁸ 街⁹—⁸*ta-*⁹*chieh* the street ⁵*shih-*⁶*fu-*⁷*ma* Shih-fu-ma ⁴*nei* inside ¹*shun-*²*chih-*³*mên* the Shun-chih Gate; "Shih-fu-ma street inside Shun-chih Gate" (73 col. 7).

十¹ 年² 之³ 內⁴—⁴*nei* in the inside ³*chih* of ¹*shih* ten ²*nien* years, *i.e.* within ten years (164).

城¹ 外²—²*wai* in the outside ¹*ch'êng* of the city, *i.e.* outside the city.

安 定 門 外 *an-ting mên wai* outside the An-ting Gate (68; *cf.* 78 cols. 9 and 10).

數¹ 百² 里³ 之⁴ 外⁵—⁵*wai* in the outside ⁴*chih* of ¹*shu* several ²*pai* hundred ³*li* Li, *i.e.* more than several hundred Li (20).

五¹ 口² 之³ 外⁴—⁴*wai* ³*chih* outside, besides ¹*wu* ²*k'ou* the five ports (21).

低¹ 窪² 間³—³*chien* at places ¹*ti* ²*wa* of low ground, *i.e.* in low land or ground (258).

民¹ 間²—²*chien* at the place ¹*min* of the people, *i.e.* with the people, among the people, a phrase which is very frequently used as simply meaning "the people" *e.g.*

所¹ 有² 民³ 間⁴ 田⁵ 地⁶—¹*so-*²*yu* the ⁵*t'ien-*⁶*ti* land of ³*min-*⁴*chien* "among the people," *i.e.* the people (237; *cf.* 242 col. 9; 251 col. 4; 271 col. 11).

夜¹ 間²—²chien at the time ¹yeh of the night, i.e at night time, during the night (73).

閏二月間 jun êrh-yüeh chien, during the second intercalary month (154).

午間 wu-chien, at noon.

八¹ 月² 初³ 間⁴—⁴chien at, during ³ch'u the beginning (i.e. the first ten days) ¹pa²yüeh of the eighth month (231).

夏間—hsia-chien, at summer time (234).

刑¹ 部² 後³—³hou behind, at the back of ¹hsing-²pu the Office of the Board of Punishments (82).

數¹ 十 餘³ 命⁴ 之⁵ 多⁶—⁶to the quantity ⁵chih of (i.e. AS MANY AS) ³yü over ¹shu several times ²shih ten ⁴ming human lives (280; cf. 270 col. 5); but

一百多人 yi pai to jên MORE than 100 men.

(39) These *post*positions are frequently preceded by *pre*positions, and in such cases, according to the rule above explained, the genitive stands between the preposition and the noun representing the postposition. Thus 中 *chung* may be preceded by 在 *tsai*, in, at; 內 *nei*, by 於 *yü*, in, at; 外 *wai* by 除 *ch'u*, besides, etc.

在水中 tsai-shui-chung, within the water, under water (122; cf. 124 col. 3; 105 col. 12).

於¹ 三² 年³ 期⁴ 內⁵—¹yü-⁵nei within ⁴ch'i the limit ²san-³nien of three years (80).

於¹ 夾² 衣³ 褲⁴ 內⁵—¹yü-⁵nei in, within ²chia-³i-⁴k'u double upper garments and trowsers, i.e. clothes lined with bags. "Concealed in the lining of their upper garments or trowsers" (103).

於¹ 保² 甲³ 章⁴ 程⁵ 之⁶ 內⁷—¹yü-⁶chih-⁷nei in ²pao-³chia-⁴chang-⁵ch'êng the regulations affecting the tithing system (106).

於¹ 一² 月³ 之⁴ 內⁵—¹yü-⁴chih-⁵nei in, within ²yi-³yüeh one month (221).

除¹ 收² 之³ 外⁴—¹ch'u-⁴wai besides ²shou-³chih what had been received,—"over and above what he had received" (55).

The phrase 除 ... 外, ch'u ... wai, is very frequently used to include complete sentences, with which form I shall deal on another occasion.

(40) The genitive by position as well as when formed by 之 chih is used for the expression of fractional numbers. This it appears is an elliptic form of a phrase like 十¹ 分² 之³ 一⁴ ⁴yi one ³chih of ¹shih ten ²fên parts, i.e. one tenth (306); by omitting 分 fên the above fraction may be expressed by 十 之 一 shih chih yi=one tenth; 十 之 七 八 shih chih ch'i pa=seven or eight tenths (253 col. 10; cf. 347 cols. 8. and 9).

(41) The relation between a genitive and the noun upon which it is dependent may seem to be inverted in Chinese, when compared to the usage of the English and other Western languages. We say "ten thousand kinds of difficulties," the Chinese say "difficulties of ten thousand kinds;" they say "the plough land of an inch" instead of "an inch of plough-land," etc., as may be seen from the following examples.

萬¹ 種² 艱³ 難⁴—³chien-⁴nan difficulties ¹wan ²chung of ten thousand kinds, i.e. "every sort of difficulty."

一¹ 寸² 之³ 土⁴ 田⁵—⁴t'u ⁵t'ien the plough-land ³chih of ¹yi ²ts'un one inch, i.e. "an inch of plough-land" (124 col. 9).

(42) A personal pronoun placed in the genitive, either by position or with 之 chih, becomes a possessive pronoun.

伊 i he, she, etc.; 伊¹ 父²—¹i of him ²fu the father, i.e. "his father" (399).

伊¹ 之² 勇³—¹i ²chih his ³yung braves (398).

吾 *wu*, I, me, my; 吾弟 *wu ti*, my younger brother, *i.e.* "you" in addressing a junior (330 col. 12; 336 col. 5).

吾兄 *wu hsiung*, my elder brother, *i.e.* "you" in addressing a senior (374 col. 3; 378 col. 12).

我 *wo* I, we. 我軍 *wo chün*, my troops; our troops (393 col. 10).

我中土 *wo chung t'u*, our middle land, our China (317).

我船 *wo ch'uan* our ships (320 col. 1; *cf.* 376 col. 10).

(43) The above examples represent cases in which the expression placed in the genitive consists of a single noun or term. We have now to proceed to such cases, very important in Chinese, in which ante-position or the use of 之 *chih* is resorted to, in order to express the genitive of a complete sentence. The genitive may in such cases come to express what in other languages is represented by temporal, relative, interrogative, etc., clauses, by the genitive of gerunds in Latin or by some other combined syntactical form of speech.

A similarity to the genitive of gerunds may be discovered in examples like the following:—

弭¹盜²安³良⁴之⁵善⁶政⁷—⁶*shan* a good ⁷*chêng* government measure ⁵*chih* of, for ¹*mi* suppressing ²*tao* robbers, and ³*an* making easy ⁴*liang* the good, loyal subjects; "the best of government measures for the repression of brigandage and the preservation unharmed of the well-disposed" (106).

安¹民²之³良⁴法⁵—⁴*liang* a good ⁵*fa* method ³*chih* of, for ¹*an* making easy ²*min* the people. "An excellent measure for the security of the people" (109 cols. 5 and 12; *cf.* 445 col. 8).

開¹自²新³之⁴路⁵—¹*k'ai* to open ⁵*lu* the way ⁴*chih* of ³*hsin* renewing ²*tzŭ* one's self, *i.e.* "to give one a chance of amending" (113).

行¹團²練³之⁴法⁴—⁵*fa* the method, system ⁴*chih* of ¹*hsing* acting, working ²*t'uan-lien* militia, train-bands (113).

無¹ 買² 食³ 鴉⁴ 片⁵ 烟⁶ 甘⁷ 結⁸—⁷kan-⁸chieh a bond for ¹wu not ²mai buying and ³shih smoking ⁴ya-⁵p'ien-⁶yen Opium (236).

(44) A complete sentence made dependent upon a noun expressing time or a division of time, usually takes the place of what in Western languages is represented by a temporal clause, e.g.

徐¹ 珍² 家³ 被⁴ 盜⁵ 之⁶ 時⁷—⁷shih at the time ⁶chih of ⁵chia the house of ¹hsü-²chên Hsü Chên ⁴pei-⁵tao suffering robbery, being robbed, i.e. "WHEN the house of Hsü Chên was robbed" (286; cf. 249 col. 8; 349 col. 4).

利¹ 限² 到³ 日⁴—⁴jih on the day of ²hsien the limit of ¹li the interest ³tao arriving, i.e. "WHEN the term for payment of interest had expired" (68).

委¹ 員² 查³ 報⁴ 之⁵ 後⁶—⁶hou in the after time ⁵chih of ¹wei-²yüan the Wei-yüan's, the Deputy's ³ch'a-⁴pao reporting, i.e. "AFTER the Wei-yüan has reported" (268).

(45) Such nouns expressing time are very frequently preceded by a preposition or some other word having reference to them, when, by the rule above explained, the sentence (here representing a genitive) is placed between the noun and the preposition. Thus 時 shih, time, or 日 jih, day, may be connected with 於 yü, or 當 tang, at, in, or 臨 lin, expressing simultaneousness, or 每 mei, each, always; 後 hou, after time, may be connected with 於 yü, in, at, 自 tzŭ' from, since, 俟 ssŭ, to wait, waiting, hence "not until," "as soon as," "when"; etc.

於 進 口 之 時 "when entering port."

當¹ 價² 昂³ 之⁴ 時⁵—¹tang ⁵shih at the time ⁴chih of ³ang the rising of ²chia the price, i.e. WHEN the price rises (242).

每¹ 於² 對³ 仗⁴ 之⁵ 時⁶—¹mei always ²yü ⁶shih at the time ⁵chih of ³tui-⁴chang fighting, i.e. "WHENEVER fighting takes place" (397; cf. 248 col. 11).

於¹ 黎² 革³ 後⁴ 身⁵ 故⁶—⁵*shên* ⁶*ku* he died ¹*yü* in ⁴*hou* the after time of ²*ts'an* ³*ko* the depriving of rank, *i.e.* "he died AFTER he had been deprived of his rank" (294).

自¹ 賣² 之³ 後⁴—¹*tzŭ* from ⁴*hou* the after time ³*chih* of ²*mai* selling, "from the time of sale" (85; *cf.* 68 col. 11).

於¹ 到² 甯³ 之⁴ 日⁵—¹*yü* at, on ⁵*jih* the day ⁴*chih* of ²*tao* arriving ³*ning* at Ningpo, "on (his) arrival at Ningpo" (4).

於¹ 洋² 船³ 未⁴ 經⁵ 進⁶ 口⁷ 之⁸ 前⁹—¹*yü* in, at ⁹*ch'ien* the foretime ⁸*chih* of ²*yang*-³*ch'uan* foreign vessels ⁴*wei* not ⁵*ching* (sign of the past) having ⁶*chin* entered ⁷*k'ou* port, *i.e.* "before foreign vessels have entered port" (248). Note the use of the negative particle ⁴*wei* in the preceding sentence, an idiom of the Chinese language. The Chinese say "previous to the Southern Ocean's *not* being prohibited" instead of "previous to its being prohibited", *i.e.* closed to trade.

南¹ 洋² 未³ 禁⁴ 之⁵ 先⁶,—⁶*hsien* in the fore time ⁵*chih* of ¹*nan*-²*yang* the Southern Ocean's ³*wei* not ⁴*chin* being prohibited, *i.e.* "previous to the Southern Ocean being closed to emigration" (317).

未¹ 到² 之³ 前⁴ 二⁵ 日⁶—⁴*ch'ien* in the fore time ³*chih* of ¹*wei* not ²*tao* arriving, ⁵*êrh* (by) two ⁶*jih* days, *i.e.* "two days before his arrival" (339).

(46) The genitive (with or without 之 *chih*) of a complete sentence is very frequently employed to form what in Western languages would be expressed by a relative clause or a participial phrase.

未¹ 收² 之³ 洋⁴ 銀⁵ 一⁶ 千⁷ 九⁸ 百⁹ 元¹⁰—the ⁶*yi*-⁷*ch'ien*-⁸*chiu*-⁹*pai*, one thousand nine hundred ¹⁰*yüah* dollars of ⁴*yang*-⁵*yin* foreign money ³*chih* of ¹*wei* not ²*shou* receiving, *i.e.* "the 1,900 dollars which have not been received," or "the 1,900 dollars still unpaid" (55; *cf.* 4 col. 12; 21 col. 1; 101 col. 5; 200 col. 7).

英¹ 國² 公³ 館⁴ 需⁵ 用⁶ 物⁷ 件⁸—⁷wu ⁸chien articles ("that are to be," expressed by position) ⁵hsü-⁶yung used by ¹ying ²kuo ³kung ⁴kuan the British Legation house, "Stores for the British Legation" (47).

毋¹ 逸² 特³ 示⁴—³t'ê a special ⁴shih proclamation ("which" expressed by position) ¹wu must not ²wei be disregarded (438).

(47) The relative pronoun 所 so is frequently added in such sentences without altering the position of words; it forms part of the sentence made dependent upon a noun by position or the use of 之 chih.

該¹ 犯² 係³ 其⁴ 所⁵ 生⁶ 之⁷ 子⁸,—¹kai the ²fan criminal ³hsi is, was ⁸tzŭ the son ⁵so ⁷chih (expressing the relative connection:) whom ⁴ch'i she ⁶shêng had borne. "The homicide was her own born son" (203).

(48) To understand a relative clause formed by the combined use of 所 so and the genitive (by position or with 之 chih), it is important to know that the subject of the clause is placed before, and the verb after, the word 所 so (cf. Julien p. 96: "Monographie de So,"), and that the noun upon which a relative clause is dependent, stands at the end. For instance:

糧¹ 船² 所³ 過⁴ 地⁵ 方⁶,—does not mean: "the grain vessels which cross the place," but: ⁵ti-⁶fang the place, or places ³so which ¹liang-²ch'uan the grain vessels ⁴kuo cross, or pass; "the places crossed by the grain vessels" (280).

其¹ 所² 遺³ 兵⁴ 棧⁵ 等⁶ 房⁷,—the ⁴ping soldiers, and ⁵chan godown ⁶têng (expressing the plurality of kinds of houses, but here not generalising) ⁷fang houses ²so (in connection with the genitive by position) which ¹ch'i they ³i left behind; i.e. "the barracks and storehouses they left behind" (22; cf. 294 col. 2).

(49) The general relative pronoun 凡 fan, may stand at

the head of such a genitive, when the force of the Latin *quisquis* or *quicumque*, if not *omnis*, is to be given to the clause, as in,

凡¹ 同² 籍³ 之⁴ 人⁵—¹*fan* ⁴*chih* quicunque ⁵*jèn* homines ²*hui* ³*chi* domum redeunt; "any person who does return home" (130).

(50) The Genitive (with or without 之 *chih*) of a complete sentence may express various relations which it would be difficult or impracticable to bring under any grammatical head, such as clauses containing indirect questions, or even clauses which, regular though they may seem to the Chinese mind, we cannot explain but as decidedly elliptic. The translation, of course, varies in all these cases and must often necessarily deviate from the literal text.

毋¹ 論² 何³ 處⁴ 之⁵ 兵⁶—⁶*ping* the soldiers ⁵*chih* of ¹*wu-*²*lun* it does not matter ³*ho* what ⁴*ch'u* place, *i.e.* the soldiers of any place (98).

所¹ 有² 審³ 明⁴ 定⁵ 擬⁶ 緣⁷ 由⁸—¹*so-*²*yu* the ⁷*yüan-*⁸*yu* circumstances of ³*shèn-*⁴*ming* investigating and ⁵*ting-*⁶*i* giving judgment, *i.e.* "particulars connected with the trial and award" (204; *cf.* 149 col. 1; 238 col. 12; 240 col. 7).

(51) A sort of elliptic construction becomes necessary and is very frequent if a law, a statute, an article of treaty, a rule or regulation is quoted, when the sentence shortly describing the contents of the law, statute, etc., is made dependent (by genitive with or without 之 *chih*) upon such words as 律 *lü* and 例 *li*, law, statute, 欵 *k'uan*, 條 *t'iao*, etc., article, paragraph, and others.

刑¹ 部² 引³ 子⁴ 毆⁵ 父⁶ 毋⁷ 殺⁸ 者⁹ 凌¹⁰ 遲¹¹ 處¹² 死¹³ 律¹⁴ ¹*hsing-*²*pu* the Board of Punishment ³*yin* adduce, quote, ¹⁴*lü* the law (⁴ to ¹³representing the contents of the law, *viz.*, that of) ⁴*tzǐ* children, ⁵*ou* beating ⁶*fu* father or ⁷*mu* mother, ⁹*chè* those who ⁸*sha* kill, ¹⁰*ling-*¹¹*ch'ih* being cut to pieces, ¹²*ch'u* are awarded [13]ssŭ death, execution. "The Board of Punishments cite the statute condemning any child that gives a blow that proves fatal to father or mother, to death by slow degrees" (202).

照[1] 威[2] 偪[3] 人[4] 致[5] 死[6] 律[7]—chao according to [7]lü the law (of, concerning, treating on, "holding out punishment for," or something of the kind) [2]wei [3]fu intimidating and urging, ill-using [4]jên a man [5]chih so that [6]ssŭ he die. "Under the statute punishing persons who occasion the death of others by deeds or words acting on their fears or feelings" (180).

照[1] 盜[2] 决[3] 河[4] 防[5] 之[6] 律[7]—[1]chao according to [7]lü the law [6]chih of, "against" [2]tao clandestinely, unlawfully [3]chüeh breaking open [5]fang the dykes of [4]ho rivers. "Under the law against unlawful opening of river works" (125; cf. 255 cols. 4 and 6; 180 col. 9; 196 cols. 9 and 10).

照[1] 地[2] 丁[3] 錢[4] 糧[5] 例[6]—[1]chao according to [6]li the statute (of "regulating the collection of") [2]ti-[3]ting [4]ch'ien-[5]liang the Land Tax (106; cf. 180 col. 3; 432 col. 7; etc).

田[1] 地[2] 入[3] 官[4] 之[5] 條[6]—[6]t'iao a paragraph [5]chih of, "threatening, holding out," [3]ju [4]kuan confiscation of [1]t'ien-[2]ti the land (here of land, on which poppy was grown, 247 col. 2).

(52) As a general rule, complete sentences, more especially, when long and complicated, are in the business style, found to be made dependent (with or without 之 chih) upon certain abstract nouns, the translation of which, if not suppressed altogether, varies very much according to circumstances. Amongst the nouns most frequently used in the manner indicated, is 事 shih, affairs, matters. The example 通[1] 商[2] 之[3] 事[4]—[4]shih matters [3]chih of [1]t'ung-[2]shang foreign trade,* "treaty matters," (3 col. 5)—shows 事 shih in

* 商通 t'ung-shang is a technical term for all trade carried on under the treaties concluded between China and Foreign countries; hence 通商之事, "treaty matters," 通商various口, "the Treaty Ports."

combination with a single term or noun, and in such cases it is easily rendered. It becomes almost untranslateable in the very common phrase 爲 照 會 事, *wei chao-hui shih*, "in the matter of an official communication," which we may look upon as the stereotyped introductory sentence of all official documents. Documents, whether despatches between equals or officials of different rank, or petitions, proclamations, etc., are generally headed by the name and official title of the writer, or the writers if more than one, followed by a phrase corresponding to the above.

欽¹ 差² 大³ 臣⁴ 者⁵ 爲⁶ 照⁷ 會⁸ 事⁹—the ¹*ch'in* Imperial ²*ch'ai* envoy and ³*ta*-⁴*ch'ên* Minister of State ⁵*ch'i* Ch'i (Kiying) ⁶*wei* on behalf of ⁹*shih* the affair of ⁷*chao*-⁸*hui* a despatch,—which sentence may be looked at as the heading of the document and rendered: "A despatch from the Imperial Envoy, etc., Kiying." (3 col. 3; *cf.* 4 col. 6; 5 col. 8; 7 col. 8; etc.)

If the despatch in question is a reply to a despatch received from an equal, the term 照 復 *chao-fu* appears in the place of 照 會 *chao-hui* (10 col. 9; 12 col. 3; etc.); if a despatch from a superior to an inferior, the term 札 行 *cha-hsing*; if a reply from a superior 札 復 *cha-fu*; if a communication exchanged between Chinese officials of equal rank, 移 咨 *i-tsŭ* (32 col. 4; 34 col. 4; 36 col. 3; etc.); if a communication sent by express, 飛 移 *fei-i* (98 col. 5); if a proclamation, 曉 諭 *hsiao-yü* (419 col. 12; 422 col. 10; 426 col. 12; 433 col. 1); 示 遵 *shih-ts'un* (440 col. 11), and other terms descriptive of the kind of document issued.* Additions containing allusions to the general purpose of the document or other extensions frequently appear between 爲 *wei* and 事 *shih, e.g.*

* I do not enter here upon the terminology of official forms, such being not immediately connected with the subject in hand.

署¹ 南²海³ 縣⁴ 左⁵堂⁶ 施⁷ 爲⁸ 剴⁹ 切¹⁰ 曉¹¹ 諭¹² 以¹³ 防¹⁴ 火¹⁵ 患¹⁶ 事¹⁷—¹*shu* the acting ⁵*tso-*⁶*t'ang* left hall, *i.e.* Assistant Magistrate of ⁴*hsien* the district of ²*nan-*³*hai* Nan-hai ⁷*shih* Shih (name) ⁸*wei* ¹⁷*shih* on account of the affair of (all that stands between ⁸*wei* and ¹⁷*shih*; viz.) ⁹*kai-*¹⁰*ch'ieh* an urgent ¹¹*hsiao-*¹²*yü* proclamation ¹³*i* in order to, for the purpose of ¹⁴*fang* guarding against ¹⁶*huan* the calamity of ¹⁵*huo* fire, *i.e.* "the Assistant Magistrate *Shih* issues an urgent proclamation for the prevention of fire" (442; *cf.* 447 col. 12).

Similarly we find in the introductory sentence, or preamble as we may fitly call it, the phrase 爲¹ 嚴² 禁³ 事⁴, so and so, ¹*wei* on behalf of ⁴*shih* an affair of ²*yen* strictly ³*chin* forbidding, *i.e.* issues a prohibitory notice, or as we may put it, "A prohibitory notice issued by so and so," looking at all that proceeds 事 *shih* as a sort of heading of the document. (415; *cf.* 430 col. 2, where the word 爲 *wei* should be supplied in the text; 431 col. 7; 437 col. 6.)

爲¹ 勸² 諭³ 愚⁴ 民⁵ 事⁶, ¹*wei* on behalf of ⁶*shih* an affair of ²*ch'üan* exhorting and ³*yü* addressing in a proclamation ⁴*yü-*⁵*min* the stupid people, *i. e.* the ordinary people, the peasantry, those who are neither officials, nor soldiers, nor priests (423).

(53) The preamble introduced by 事 *shih* with or without 爲 *wei* very frequently contains a short *résumé*, in the most concise terms, of the subject matter and general bearing of the document, more especially so in petitions, plaints, and certain memorials to the throne. Petitions, as a rule, begin with a statement concerning the person of the petitioner, usually giving his name, and often adding his age and the district he belongs to; then follows a short statement of the subject of the petition, the *docket*, as it were, included by the words 稟 爲 *ping-wei*, petitioning on behalf, and 事 *shih*, an affair (of all that precedes).

具¹稟²人³李⁴福⁵有³稟⁷爲⁸風⁹聞¹⁰來¹¹歸¹²乞¹³給¹⁴
田¹⁵土¹⁶以¹⁷便¹⁸安¹⁹身²⁰事²¹. The ³jên man ¹chü ²ping
presenting the petition or "who presents the petition,"
⁴li-⁵fu-⁶yu Li Fu-yu, ⁷ping ⁸wei petitions on behalf of ²¹shih
an affair of ¹⁵t'ien-¹⁶t'u land ⁹fêng-¹⁰wên being rumoured
¹⁴chi to be given ¹³ch'i (when) prayed, applied for ¹¹lai-¹²kuei
on coming ¹⁷i-¹⁸pien in order to ¹⁹an make comfortable, give
rest to ²⁰shên the body, one's person; "Li Fu-yu presents a
petition regarding land which is rumoured to be given to im-
migrants on application for the purpose of settling down"
(62; cf. the preambles in papers Nos. 31 to 38).

(54) Such "dockets" may be found to appear at the head
of despatches and all similar written communications.

爲¹移²催³催⁴查⁵解⁶審⁷事⁸ (The prefect K'uei-lien)
¹wei on behalf of ⁸shih an affair of ²i-³ts'ui urging by letter
the ⁴ch'üeh-⁵ch'a truthfully enquiring and ⁶chieh-⁷shên forwarding verdict. This is the docket, as it were, of a
despatch "urging the sending forward of documents containing the minutes of an investigation to be made and judgment to be given" by the addressee (100). Matters referred
to the throne as in a memorial are similarly described at the
head of the document, as in the following examples:

奏¹爲²遵³旨⁴審⁵明⁶定⁷擬⁸具⁹奏¹⁰事¹¹, ¹tsou addres-
sing the throne ²wei on behalf of ¹¹shih an affair of ⁹chü-¹⁰tsou
presenting to the throne the ⁵shên-⁶ming investigation made
and ⁷ting-⁸i judgment given ³ts'un obeying ⁴chih the Emperor's
pleasure. "Your Majesty's servants address your Majesty;
for that, in obedience to an Imperial Rescript, a trial has
been held, a sentence awarded, and a report prepared
thereon to Your Majesty" (134).

奏¹爲²遵³旨⁴審⁵明⁶定⁷擬⁸恭⁹摺¹⁰仰¹¹祈¹²聖¹³鑒¹⁴
事¹⁵, ¹tsou addressing the throne ²wei on behalf of ¹⁵shih an
affair of ¹¹yang-¹²ch'i looking upward imploring the ¹³shêng

sacred ¹⁴*chien* mirror, glance on ⁹*kung* ¹⁰*chê* a respectful memorial on ⁵*shên*-⁶*ming* an investigation made and ⁷*ting*-⁸*i* judgment given ³*ts'un* ⁴*chih* in obedience to an Imperial Rescript, "Your Majesty's servant, etc.,—looking upward he implores the glance of your sacred Majesty upon a memorial reverently prepared, shewing that, in obedience to a Rescript of Your Majesty's, a trial has been satisfactorily concluded, and a sentence awarded" (150; *cf.* the preambles in papers Nos. 65 to 84).

(55) Among the abstract nouns upon which verbs or complete sentences are made dependent (by anteposition or the use of 之 *chih*), the following are, besides 事 *shih*, very commonly met with in the business style: 弊 *pi*, a malpractice, a nuisance; 思 *ssŭ*, thought; 心 *hsin*, intention; 虞 *yü*, calamity, danger; 計 *chi*, a contrivance, a measure, a plan; 際 *chi*, an occasion, a time (此際 *tz'ŭ chi*, this time); 勢 *shih*, condition; 舉 *chü*, an undertaking; 責 *tsê*, responsibility, duty; 由 *yu*, or 緣由 *yüan yu*, 端 *tuan*, and other terms of a similar meaning, *viz.* "circumstances, facts;" 言 *yen*, words, mention. This list may be easily increased, and as examples abound in documents relating to business, I shall confine myself to illustrating a few.

彼¹ 此² 推³ 諉⁴ 之⁵ 弊⁶,—⁶*pi* the malpractice ⁵*chih* of ¹*p'i* there and ²*tz'ŭ* here (*i.e.* on either side) ³*t'ui*-⁴*wei* backing out (158; *cf.* 118 col.10; 165 col.1; 249 col.1; 265 col. 9; 430 col. 4).

孰¹ 無² 故³ 土⁴ 之⁵ 思⁶,—¹*shu* who ²*wu* has not ⁶*ssŭ* the thought ⁵*chih* of the ³*ku* old ⁴*t'u* country? "There is not one that has forgotten his old land" (130).

以¹ 杜² 其³ 圖⁴ 鬭⁵ 之⁶ 心⁷,—¹*i* in order to ²*tu* restrict ³*ch'i* of them, their ⁷*hsin* intention, inclination ⁶*chih* of ⁴*t'u*-⁵*tou* planning fights (282).

幸¹ 無² 衝³ 決⁴ 之⁵ 虞⁶,—¹hsing fortunately ²wu there is (was) not ⁶yü the calamity of ³ch'ung-⁴chüeh a sudden rupture (of the river banks). "Happily, there has been no such calamity as a breach of either bank of the Yün Ho" (122 col. 5; cf. Wade's Note).

既¹ 無² 廢³ 業⁴ 之⁵ 虞⁶,—¹chi since ²wu there is not ⁶yü the calamity, inconvenience ⁵chih of ³fei abandoning, setting aside ⁴yeh the pursuit of business (421; cf. 171 col. 1; 448 col. 3.)

(56) The verb 思 ssŭ, to think, is, in one of the foregoing examples, made into an abstract noun, and what ought to be the object of the verb is made dependent upon this verbal noun by using the genitive. This kind of circumlocution is by no means rare in the business style and is easily understood after some practice, e.g.

因¹ 貴² 大³ 臣⁴ 來⁵ 文⁶ 有⁷ 福⁸ 州⁹ 民¹⁰ 情¹¹ 甚¹² 是¹³ 相¹⁴ 安¹⁵ 之¹⁶ 說¹⁷,—¹yin because ⁵lai-⁶wên in the despatch of ²kuei-³ta-⁴ch'ên your Excellency ⁷yu there is ¹⁷shuo the speaking, the mention made ¹⁶chih of ¹¹ch'ing the condition of ⁸fu-⁹chou ¹⁰min the people of Fu-chou ¹³shih being ¹²shên very much ¹⁴hsiang mutually ¹⁵an peaceful, i.e. "because, in your despatch, you mention that the people of Foochow are quite peacefully disposed" (18).

The verb 言 yen, to speak, is very frequently employed like 說 shuo in the preceding example; so are various other verbs, the substantival use of which gives the construction of the clause a peculiar idiomatic turn.

The Dative.

(57) Where it is at all necessary to use a dative, it is done either by position, or by the use of certain prepositions. The position of the dative has been shown above. As a rule verbs involving the giving, communicating, telling, etc., are

followed by an immediate object (accusative) representing the object given, communicated, etc., and a dative, representing the person to whom it is given, communicated, etc. The rule, with regard to the position of the two cases dependent upon the verb, has been shown to be that the dative precedes the accusative.

竊身於同治三年三月初一日憑中人管賢士
借給宛平縣吳家莊民人吳兩紋銀一百兩
"Petitioner humbly states that on the 1st day of the 3rd moon of the 3rd year of T'ung Chih, upon the representation of Kuan Hsien-shih, who acted as negotiator of the loan, he lent the sum of 100 Taels good silver (or sycee) to Wu Liang, a native of Wu Chia Chuang in the district of Wanp'ing" (68).

(58) The accusative, of course, precedes both the verb and the dative when it is expressed by 將 *chiang*.

懇¹將²徐³保⁴之⁵屋⁶字⁷田⁸園⁹給¹⁰予¹¹蟻¹²等¹³居¹⁴
住¹⁵耕¹⁶種¹⁷—(Petitioners) ¹*k'ĕn* pray to ¹⁰*chi*-¹¹*yü* give (verb) ¹²*i*-¹³*têng* them, the petitioners (dative) ²*chiang* (sign of the accusative) ⁶*wu*-⁷*yü* the house and ⁸*t'ien*-⁹*yüan* garden ⁵*chih* of ³*hsü*-⁴*pao* Hsü Pao ¹⁴*chü*-¹⁵*chu* to live in and ¹⁶*kêng*-¹⁷*chung* plough and plant, *i.e.* carry on agriculture. "They would implore [Your Excellency] to bestow on your Petitioners the house and land [left by] Hsü Pao" (63).

(59) The most common preposition used for the expression of the dative, in the business style, is 與 *yü*, properly a verb meaning "to give;" hence it is used after all verbs involving a communication, real or verbal, and often corresponds to 給 *kei* of the mandarin colloquial.

賣¹與²李³九⁴老⁵爺⁶—¹*mai* to sell ²*yü* to ⁵*lao*-⁶*yeh* Mr. ³*li chiu* Li Chiu (85 ; *cf.* 82 col. 12 ; 83 col. 11).

交與 *chiao yü*, to hand over, to give "to" (382 col. 7).

該¹ 處² 地³ 保⁴ 與⁵ 身⁶ 家⁷ 送⁸ 信⁹—³ti-⁴pao the Ti-pao (policeman) of ¹kai the ²ch'u place ⁸sung sent ⁹hsin a letter, "word" ⁵yü to ⁶shên my ⁷chia family (69). Note that the dative here precedes the verb.

(60) As in Greek, verbs or adjectives expressing sameness similarity, accordance, etc., and their opposites, are connected with the dative case, the person or object compared being preceded by the particle 與 yü.

與¹ 該² 弁³ 等⁴ 所⁵ 稟⁶ 畧⁷ 同⁸—⁷lio on the whole ⁸t'ung the same ¹yü as ⁵so that which ²kai the said ⁸pien-⁴têng officers ⁶ping state; "being on the whole identical with what those officers stated" (394).

與¹ 原² 議³ 不⁴ 符⁵—⁴pu not ⁵fu agreeing ¹yü with ²yüan the original ³i understanding (56).

與¹ 良² 民³ 無⁴ 異⁵—⁴wu not having ⁵i difference, i.e. not different ¹yü from ²liang good ³min people, subjects; "being well disposed like other good subjects" (308).*

(61) The preposition 向 hsiang, "towards," often expresses relations of a noun which correspond to the dative, sometimes also to the accusative case, especially before verbs implying a communication, real or verbal, such as "to say, to state, to ask for, to blame" or "to beat, to strike."

彭¹ 德² 州³ 向⁴ 孫⁵ 惟⁶ 鑾⁷ 回⁸ 復⁹—¹p'êng-²tê-³chou P'êng Tê-chou ⁸hui returned, carried back ⁹fu the answer ⁴hsiang to ⁵sun-⁶wei-⁷luan Sun Wei-luan (178).

向¹ 張² 餘³ 祥⁴ 告⁵ 述⁶—He ⁵kao-⁶shu reported ¹hsiang to ²chang ³yü-⁴hsiang Chang Yü-hsiang (200).

* In the case of 異 i, "different from," and the cognate terms, the object compared may also be preceded by 於 yü, which corresponds to the Latin quam after comparatives, e.g. 異¹ 於² 常³ 年⁴—¹i different ²yü from ³ch'ang ordinary ⁴nien years (122). Note that 於 yü follows, while 與 yü precedes, the term of comparison. The example given above might also read 無 異 於 良 民, without the sense being different.

向¹ 父² 揑³ 稱⁴—He ³nieh falsely ⁴ch'ëng, stated ¹hsiang to ²fu his father (200).

向¹ 其² 查³ 問⁴—il ¹hsiang ²ch'i leur ³ch'a-⁴wên demanda, viz., le passe-port; "he asked them for the passport" (48).

向¹ 往² 來³ 行⁴ 路⁵ 之⁶ 人⁷ 乞⁸ 討⁹ 錢¹⁰ 文¹¹—⁸ch'i-⁹t'ao demander ⁷jên aux hommes (dative) ²wang³lai ⁴hsing ⁵lu ⁶chih passant par le chemin ¹⁰ch'ien ¹¹wên des sapèques. "Vorübergehenden (dative) Geld abverlangen" (431; cf. 289 col. 3; 209 col. 3; 199 col. 9; 211 col. 5; 189 col. 11; 184 cols. 3; and 7; 192 col. 10).

(62) It is under this head, too, that I have to mention the verbs meaning "to borrow," as money, the person *from* whom the money, etc., is borrowed being introduced with 向 *hsiang*, before the verb. In this case *hsiang* does not, in English, correspond to either dative or accusative, but simply indicates verbal communication necessitating an approach.

向¹ 李² 祥³ 借⁴ 用⁵ 錢⁶ 文⁷—he ⁴chieh borrowed ⁵yung for use ⁶ch'ien ⁷wên money ¹hsiang from ²li ³hsiang Li Hsiang, asked Li Hsiang to lend him some money" (177).

向¹ 伊² 嫂³ 借⁴ 取⁵ 燈⁶ 油⁷ 不⁸ 給⁹—he ⁴chieh ⁵ch'ü borrowed ¹hsiang from ²i his ³sao elder brother's wife ⁶têng-⁷yu lamp-oil, and ⁸pu ⁹chi was not given, did not receive it. "Being refused some lamp-oil that he asked from his elder brother's wife" (202; cf. 223 col. 9; 224 col. 6).

(63) In order to commit the act of striking, etc., one has to bodily approach the object; hence the use of 向 *hsiang* in connection with such verbs.

向¹ 門² 官³ 揮⁴ 鞭⁵ 毆⁶ 打⁷,— They ⁴hui ⁵pien horsewhipped and ⁶ou ⁷ta violently assailed ¹hsiang ²mên ³kuan the gate officer (49).

取¹ 土² 坯³ 向⁴ 白⁵ 萬⁶ 氏⁷ 擲⁸ 毆⁹, Ho ¹ch'ü picked up ²t'u ³p'ei a clod and ⁸chih ⁹ou flung it violently ⁴hsiang at ⁷shih the (married) woman ⁵pai ⁶ko Pai Ko (202).

In the above example 向 *hsiang* is used in its proper meaning as a preposition, *viz.* "towards, against, at," and shows how in the case of verbs having a cognate meaning as "to hurt by throwing, beating, pushing," etc., it may come to represent the object (accusative or dative) dependent upon the same.

(64) In a great many cases the object following a verb of a certain meaning is expressed by the dative in one, and the accusative in another European language. As Chinese writers are not, of course, any more conscious of the logical difference existing between the first and second *"me"* in the two examples "give *me*" and "kill *me*," it appears to be superfluous to pursue this subject in a more detailed manner. The German verb "befehlen" (to order) is followed by the dative, while its Latin equivalent "jubere" governs the accusative. In Chinese the verb 飭 *ch'ih*, "to order," and verbs of cognate meaning, are simply followed by an object, and in the absence of all distinguishing forms, it would be immaterial to assign this object to either the one or the other of the two cases.

Pronouns.

Personal Pronouns.

(65) In Chinese the use of personal pronouns is much more restricted than it is in any Western language of the present day, and, as of the verb nothing but that part is expressed which, in a Latin or Greek verb, corresponds to the root, this part of speech has to be supplied entirely from the general context. The economy in their use seems to be outweighed by the number of words at the disposal of the language for expressing *ego, tu ille,* etc. Speaking of Chinese in general we find the following words in use as personal pronouns.

1. Pronouns of the first person:
I, ME; WE, US, etc.
} 朕 chên; 我 wo; 予 'yü; 吾 wu; 余 yü; 俺 an; 咱 tsa.

2. Pronouns of the second person:
THOU, THEE; YOU, etc.
} 爾 êrh; 而 êrh; 如 ju; 汝 ju; 女 ju; 若 jo; 你 ni.

3. Pronouns of the third person:
HE, HIM; THEY, THEM, etc.
} 其 ch'i; 之 chih; 厥 chüeh; 伊 i; 他 t'a.

A few of these are, however, confined to the ancient style, or are only exceptionally met with in texts written in the business language, as 汝 ju; while others are peculiar to the Mandarin colloquial and, therefore, may occur in novels written in that style, or—as is sometimes the case—in depositions, when the very words used by a witness (who of course spoke colloquial) are to be quoted.

(66) The personal pronouns chiefly used in the business style are 我 wo and 吾 wu for the first person, 爾 êrh, for the second, and 伊 i, 其 ch'i and 厥 chüeh for the third person. 朕 chên, I, We [the *pluralis majestaticus*], it is the privilege of the Emperor to use when speaking of his person, and occurs only in Imperial Edicts and similar documents. This restriction on the use of *chên* which, in the Shuking, is still used by persons of an exalted position in general, dates as far back as the *Ch'in Shih-huang-ti* at the close of the third century B.C.

(67) The plural of pronouns if expressed at all is formed by affixing 等 têng or 輩 pei.

(68) A personal pronoun placed before a noun, and thus becoming a genitive by position, receives the force of a possessive pronoun.

我 wo, I, WE, etc.

(69) 我 wo is more frequently met with in the sense of *noster* than in that of *ego*, the usual meaning of this word when standing alone, in the colloquial language.*

我¹ 兩² 國³—¹wo our ²liang two ³kuo countries, i.e. both our countries (13 col. 12; 17 col. 8).

我中土 wo chung t'u, our middle land, our China (317).

我順德邑城 wo shun-tê i-ch'êng, our city of Shun-tê (443).

我船 wo ch'uan our ships (320).

我軍 wo chün our troops, also: my troops (393 col. 10; cf. 376 col. 10).

我輩 wo pei } we; see above under "Plural".
我等 wo têng }

老¹ 弟² 愛³ 我⁴ 至⁵ 深⁶—¹lao-²ti the old brother, i.e. you ³ai love, like ⁴wo me ⁵chih-⁶shên very much (339 col. 11).

吾 wu, I, ME, etc.

(70) 吾 wu it is justly remarked by Endlicher (p. 249) is chiefly used as a singular. It is is very common as a possessive in the phrases:

吾兄 wu hsiang, my elder brother, i.e. you (said to a senior; 374 col. 1 seqq.); and 吾弟 wu ti, my younger brother, i.e. you (said to a junior; 336 col. 5).

爾 êrh, You.

(71) This character chiefly occurs in proclamations when the people are addressed. It is never used to equals in correspondence (cf. Wade, Note 58 to Paper 61).

* Attention has been drawn to the composition of this character with the radical 手 shou, "hand," and the phonetic ko 戈, "a lance," which produces the original meaning of "id quod manu cepi=possideo," i.e. the meaning of a possessive pronoun. See C. MERZ, *De Pronominum Primae Personae in Libris* 書經 et 詩經 *Usu*. Vienna, 1882, p. 11.

爲¹ 此² 剴³ 切⁴ 曉⁵ 諭⁶ 爾⁷ 士⁸ 民⁹ 等¹⁰ [The Prefect] ¹wei on account of ²tz‘ŭ this ³kai-⁴ch‘ieh⁵ hsiao-⁶yü makes a distinct proclamation to ⁷êrh you, ⁸shih the literati and ⁹min the people ¹⁰têng (sign of the plural) (110).

爾¹ 等² 在³ 番⁴ 貿⁵ 易⁵ 良⁷ 民⁸—¹êrh-²têng you (Plural) ³tsai in ⁴fan foreign countries ⁵mao-⁶yi trading ⁷liang good ⁸min people. "You, good subjects trading abroad" (130).

爾輩 êrh-pei, people of your kind, i.e. you (Plural; 120 col. 3).

(72) 爾 êrh, in some cases, receives the force of a particle of affirmation and may, if at all, be translated by "really, indeed." This change from its original meaning reminds one of the Homeric τοι, the so called *Dativus Ethicus* of the Pronoun of the second person.

不¹ 但² 不³ 以⁴ 理⁵ 論⁶ 竟⁷ 爾⁸ 出⁹ 言¹⁰ 混¹¹ 賴¹²—he ¹pu not ²tan only ³pu did not ⁴i use ⁵li-⁶lun reasoning ⁷ching but ⁸êrh indeed ⁹ch‘u uttering ¹⁰yen words ¹¹hun-¹²lai abused. He "not only would have no amicable discussion about the matter, but was grossly abusive" (69; cf. Wade, Note 13 to Paper 39).

汝 *ju*, ʏou.

(73) This character is occasionally employed like 爾 êrh in proclamations e.g. 汝¹ 等² 愚³ 民⁴ ¹ju-²têng you ³yü-⁴min, *lit.* stupid people, *i.e.* you, the common people (as opposed to the soldiery and officials; 424 col. 12; cf. 425 cols. 2 and 9).

伊 *i*, Hᴇ, sʜᴇ, ᴇᴛᴄ.

(74) This is the word commonly used in documents when the personal pronoun of the third person is to be expressed; it stands for *he, she, him, her*; with 等 *têng*, for *they* and *them*; and as a genitive by position for *his, her* and *their*.

伊¹ 尚² 以³ 好⁴ 言⁵ 搪⁶ 塞⁷—¹i he ²shang still ³i using ⁴hao good, fair ⁵yen words ⁶t‘ang-⁷sai put him off. "He kept him at bay with fair words" (69).

乃¹ 伊² 覷³ 身⁴ 老⁵ 朽⁶ 無⁷ 能⁸,—¹*nai* then, when ²*i* he ³*shih* saw ⁴*shên* me (my being) ⁵*lao-*⁶*hsiu* old and broken and ⁷*wu* not having ⁸*nêng* power, strength. "When he saw that petitioner was a broken old man of no strength" (69).

拜¹ 伊² 為³ 師⁴ They ¹*pai* worshipped ²*i* him ³*wei* as ⁴*shih* master; "paid him the honours as master" (209).

身¹ 與² 伊³ 理⁴ 論⁵—¹*shên* I ⁴*li-*⁵*lun* reasoned ²*yü* with ³*i* him.

伊¹ 等² 逃³ 出⁴—¹*i-*²*têng* they ⁴*t'ao-*⁴*ch'u* ran out, escaped (400).

因¹ 岳² 可³ 維⁴ 曾⁵ 談⁶ 論⁷ 伊⁸ 等⁹ 行¹⁰ 兇¹¹ 生¹² 事¹³—¹*yin* because ²*yo-*³*k'o-*⁴*wei* Yo K'o-wei had ⁵*hui* together (with him) ⁶*t'an-*⁷*lun* discussed ⁸*i-*⁹*têng* their ¹⁰*hsing-*¹¹*hsiung* doing the murder and ¹²*shêng* ¹³*shih* creating the matter. "Because Yo K'o-wei had been discussing (with him) their having committed the murder and created the crime" (192).

伊 父 *i fu* his father (289 col. 1).

伊 夫 *i fu* her husband (37 col. 4).

其 *ch'i*, HE, SHE, IT; THEY, ETC.

(75) This character is very commonly used in the business style as a pronoun of the third person, and is by no means confined to the *Ku-wên* as Endlicher says it is (p. 253).

其 *ch'i*, as the representative of a pronoun, may be said to be chiefly applied in two senses. It may either refer to something preceding, when it may be called a personal pronoun (*suus* or *ejus*), or it may refer to something following, when it assumes the force of a demonstrative pronoun. In the former sense it is applied to persons as well as things, whereas 伊 *i* appears to stand for animate objects, *i.e.* men or women, only. It is hardly ever followed by the plural mark (等 *têng*, etc.), but as a genitive by position, may become a possessive pronoun.

其¹ 所² 欲³—²so that which ¹ch'i he ³yü wishes.

忖¹ 思² 船³ 上⁴ 現⁵ 有⁶ 漁⁷ 照⁸ 告⁹ 示¹⁰ 爲¹¹ 憑¹² 其¹³ 非¹⁴ 歹¹⁵ 船¹⁶ 可¹⁷ 知¹⁸—Petitioner ¹ts'un-²ssŭ considers that ³ch'uan-⁴shang on board ⁵yu there is ⁶hsien now ⁷yü-⁸chao a fishing license ⁹kao-¹⁰shih proclamation ¹¹wei as ¹²p'ing proof ¹⁷k'o can ¹⁸chih know (from which it may be known that) ¹³ch'i he, or she, i.e. his junk, ¹⁴fei is not a ¹⁵tai bad ¹⁶ch'uan ship. "Petitioner submits that appeal may be made to the proclamation notifying the issue of the fishing license, to shew that the vessel is not one engaged in unlawful proceedings" (59).

該¹ 門² 向³ 其⁴ 查⁵ 問⁶—¹kai the respective ²mên gate, gatekeeper ⁵ch'a-⁶wên asked ³hsiang (towards, here denoting object) ⁴ch'i them, viz. for their passports; ⁴ch'i here refers to three foreigners (48 col. 12).

其¹ 子²—¹ch'i of him (genitive by position), his ²tzŭ son.

父¹ 誡² 其³ 子⁴ 兄⁵ 勉⁶ 其⁷ 弟⁸—¹fu the father ²chieh exhorts ³ch'i his ⁴tzŭ son; ⁵hsiung the elder brother ⁶mien constrains ⁷ch'i his ⁸ti younger brother.

A provincial Governor has omitted to report the death of his mother. His degradation on this account is announced in the following words. 因¹ 此² 特³ 降⁴ 諭⁵ 旨⁶ 將⁷ 其⁸ 革⁹ 職¹⁰ ¹yin on account of ²tz'ŭ this, there had been ³t'ê specially ⁴chiang issued a ⁵yü-⁶chih rescript from the throne: ⁹ko-¹⁰chih cashier ⁷chiang (sign of the object) ⁸ch'i him; "a special edict has, therefore, been received from the throne ordering him to be deprived of his rank" (454).

---

(76) All these words representing personal pronouns are most sparingly used. The language is, however, in the possession of various modes of representing this class of words without taking resort to the use of any pronoun. The principal ways of thus avoiding a personal pronoun are, for instance, the repetition of the writer's

name, the *ming*; the substitution of the writer's title, especially when it is preceded by a term of modesty for the first person, or a term of honour for the second person; or the substitution of certain conventional forms coming under the category of terms of civility and etiquette.

The mentioning of the writer's name in lieu of "I, me, we," etc., is quite frequent in petitions when the *ming* is inserted in the text in characters of diminished size. The title of the writer preceded by 本 *pên*, or that of the addressee preceded by 貴 *kuei*, is chiefly used in official despatches and proclamations. A Minister of state speaking of himself says 本¹ 大² 臣³—¹*pên* this ²*ta*-³*ch'ên* minister, *i.e.* "I, the minister." Similarly we read 本 部 堂 *pên pu-t'ang*, I, the Governor General; 本 部 院 *pên pu-yüan*, I, the Governor; 本 縣 *pên hsien*, I, the District Magistrate, etc. *See* paragr. 84.

Besides these there are certain other conventional forms by which writers designate themselves. They are partly terms of modesty as *ch'ieh* 竊 "clandestine, private," or 愚 *yü*, "the stupid one" for "I," 蟻等 *i-têng*, "the ants" for "we, the petitioners." Married women style themselves 氏 *shih* in petitions; Chinese ministers addressing the throne call themselves 臣 *ch'ên*, Manchoo statesmen 奴才 *nu tsai*, *i.e.* slave, "your Majesty's slave," etc. The use of any of these many expressions depends upon occasion and custom, and demands the most careful attention on the part of writers. The etiquette to be observed in drawing up official documents is a study of its own; it is, therefore, merely alluded to as being, to a limited extent, connected with our subject.

Demonstrative Pronouns.

其 *ch'i* THIS, THAT; AS TO, AS REGARDS.

(77) We have spoken of this character as a personal pronoun of the third person. As such it occurs when referring

to something preceding it in the general context. It may still be explained as retaining this sense in combinations like 其¹ 後²—²hou in the after time ¹ch'i of it, ejus i.e. of that which precedes, i.e. "thereafter;" or 其¹ 時²,—²shih at the time ¹ch'i of it, i.e. "at that time," although even here the demonstrative force of [the word preponderates. When it refers to something following, however, ch'i becomes a demonstrative pronoun with a slight shade of the meaning of the definite article, in so far as it individualises the expression following by giving it, logically, the character of a substantive.

其¹ 未² 造³ 成⁴ 僞⁵ 銀⁶ 者⁷ 速⁸ 爲⁹ 停¹⁰ 止¹¹ 其¹² 已¹³ 造¹ 成¹⁵ 者¹⁶ 卽¹⁷ 將¹⁸ 傾¹⁹ 還²⁰ 足²¹ 紋²²—¹ch'i ⁷chê those who (giving to all that stands between the two characters the force of a substantive, a participial expression or a relative clause) ²wei have not ³ts'ao made ⁴ch'êng ready, finished ⁵wei counterfeited ⁶yin money, [should] ⁸su speedily ⁹wei–¹⁰t'ing–¹¹chih stop; ¹²ch'i ¹³chê those who ¹⁴i have ¹⁴ts'ao–¹⁵ch'êng made ready, finished ¹⁷chi at once ¹⁸chiang take (here marking the object of a noun to be supplied, viz. ⁵wei–⁶yin counterfeited money) ¹⁹ching–²⁰huan melt back into ²¹tsu–²²wên pure sycee. "Those who have not finished their counterfeitures yet should at once stop the practice; those who have got them ready should again melt them into pure sycee" (438; cf. 308 col. 5; 其 ch'i, eorum, *** 者 illi qui, i.e. those who; 309 col. 7).

(78) Chinese writers often use 其 ch'i when a new phase of an idea is entered upon, or in an enumeration of facts when we would say "finally there is," or "as to the so and so." In this sense its use resembles that of 至 chih, "as to." In the following sentence, for instance, the participial expression marked in the English version by the words "as to cases," [in brackets] is, in the Chinese text, introduced by 其 ch'i,

"Any family holding 10 *mou* is to contribute 1 *pint* per *mou*. The rate is to rise progressively; 20 *mou* holders contributing 2 pints per *mou*, 30 *mou* holders, 3 pints, and so on to 100 *mou*, holders of which will contribute, 1 peck per *mou* and there an end. [*As to cases*] where the land held is more than 100 *mou*, the amount to be contributed over and above the peck per *mou*, is not fixed, but is left to the good pleasure of the contributor" (117 col. 1 seqq).

嗣¹ 後² 細³ 磁⁴ 器⁵ 及⁶ 粗⁷ 磁⁸ 盤⁹ 碗¹⁰ 仍¹¹ 照¹² 磁¹³ 器¹⁴ 秤¹⁵ 勎¹⁶ 完¹⁷ 飹¹⁸ 其¹⁹ 極²⁰ 粗²¹ 瓦²² 器²³ 僅²⁴ 照²⁵ 佑²⁶ 價²⁷ 每²⁸ 百²⁹ 兩³⁰ 抽³¹ 稅³² 五³³ 兩³⁴—¹*ssŭ-*²*hou* hereafter ³*hsi* fine ⁴*tz'ŭ-*⁵*ch'i* chinaware ⁶*chi* and ⁷*ts'u* coarse ⁸*tz'ŭ* porcelain ⁹*p'an-*¹⁰*wan* plates and bowls [will] ¹¹*jêng* again ¹⁷*wan* pay ¹⁸*hsiang* duty ¹²*chao* according to, like ¹³*tz'ŭ-*¹⁴*ch'i* Chinaware ¹⁵*ch'êng-*¹⁶*chin* weighing catties ; ¹⁹*ch'i* [as to] the ²⁰*chi-*²¹*ts'u* coarsest ²²*wa-*²³*ch'i* pottery [will] ²⁴*chin* only ³¹*ch'ou* be levied ³²*shui* duty ²⁵*chao* according to ²⁶*ku-*²⁷*chia* value ²⁸*mei* each ²⁹*pai* hundred ³⁰*liang* taels ³³*wu* five ³⁴*liang* taels. "Fine crockery, as well as plates and dishes of coarse crockery, will continue to pay duty by weight; but the coarsest ware is to pay no more than an *ad valorem* duty of 5 per cent" (12).

In this sense 其 *ch'i* will be found to have been employed on pp. 22 col. 9; 38 col. 11; 31 col. 4; where the phrase 其餘 *ch'i yü*, "the remaining..." may be considered to explain the actual bearing of *ch'i*, standing by itself, in all similar examples; 102 col. 10; 8 col. 5 (*cf*. Wade's Note No. 24 in Paper 4, Key p. 9).

是 *shih* THIS, THAT.

(79) This is, with the following, the demonstrative pronoun chiefly used. It may mean *this* as well as *that*, whereas 此 *tz'ŭ* (hic) is employed in opposition to 彼 *p'i* (ille, illuc).

是¹ 夜² 身³ 故⁴—he ³*shên-*⁴*ku* died in ¹*shih* that ²*yeh* night (184).

是 人 *shih jên* this man.

是¹ 爲² 至³ 要⁴—¹*shih* this ²*wei* is ³*chih* most ⁴*yao* important (99).

於¹ 是² 日³—¹*yü* on ²*shih* that ³*jih* day, "on the same day."

是¹ 時²—¹*shih* this ²*shih* time; "at the same time."

(80) In connection with 以 *i*, "on account of," this pronoun forms the phrase 是 以 *shih-i*, on account of this, thereby, therefore. The preposition, in this case, follows the word governed by it. Similarly we read 何 以 *ho-i*, on account of what, what for, why. Otherwise ordinary prepositions precede *shih*. The following combinations are often met with in the business style.

於 是 *yü-shih*, on this, thereupon, thus.

如 是 *ju-shih*, 似 是 *ssŭ-shih*, like this, thus.

由 是 *yu-shih*, from this, hence.

此 *tz'ŭ*, THIS, HERE.

(81) This may be called the standard word for *this*.

此 人 *tz'ŭ jên*, this man; 此 案 *t'zŭ an*, this case; 此 次 *tz'ŭ tz'ŭ*, this time; 此 時 *tz'ŭ shih* at this time.

It also enters into combination with prepositions, *e.g.*

如 此 *ju-tz'ŭ* or 似 此 *ssŭ-tz'ŭ*, like this, thus(= 類 此 *lei-tz'ŭ*, like this, in this way; 124 col. 2).

With 等 *têng*, class, it may form the plural "these," or the indefinite pronoun *talis*, "such".

此¹ 等² 滋³ 事⁴—¹*tz'ŭ-*²*têng* these ³*tzŭ-*⁴*shih* riots (101 col. 10).

此¹ 等² 惡³ 徒⁴—¹*tz'ŭ-*²*têng* this kind of—*i.e.* such ³*ngo* bad ⁴*t'u* ruffians.

As an adverb *tz'ŭ* means "here" as apposed to "there."

在 此 *tsai-tz'ŭ*, at this place, here.

彼 *pi*, THAT, THERE.

(82) This word is chiefly used to denote the opposite of the former.

彼人 *pi jên* that man; 彼處 *pi ch'u* at that place; 彼時 *pi shih* at that time (17 col. 5).

Like the former it is used adverbially, meaning "there."

在彼 *tsai pi*, there.

It often occurs as a correlative with 此 *tz'ŭ*, the two together meaning "here and there," "on this side and on that side", *i.e.* "on either side," "both parties," "you and I."

今¹ 將² 約³ 式⁴ 繕⁵ 修⁶ 英⁷ 漢⁸ 兩⁹ 稿¹⁰ 以¹¹ 便¹² 彼¹³ 此¹⁴ 畫¹⁵ 押¹⁶ 蓋¹⁷ 印¹⁸,—¹*chin* now [we have] ⁵*shan*-⁶*hsiu* copied ²*chiang* (sign of the object) ³*yüeh*-⁴*shih* the treaty pattern (into) ⁹*liang* both ⁷*ying* English and ⁸*han* Chinese ¹⁰*kao* draughts ¹¹*i*-¹²*pien* so that ¹³*pi*-¹⁴*tz'ŭ* there and here, on both sides, by both parties [it may be] ¹⁵*hua*-¹⁶*ya* signed and ¹⁷*kai*-¹⁸*yin* sealed. "There have been prepared two copies of the treaty forwarded in draught, one in English and one in Chinese; so that the Minister and the Commissioner may sign and seal without more trouble" (15).

彼¹ 此² 議³ 定⁴—³*i* negociate and ⁴*ting* settle ¹*pi* there and ²*tz'ŭ* here; "to conclude negociations [on either side]" (15).

彼¹ 此² 素³ 有⁴ 訟⁵ 嫌⁶—¹*pi*-²*tz'ŭ* here and there, *i.e.* on both sides, there ³*su* constantly ⁴*yu* was ⁵*sung* bringing before the court and ⁶*hsien* dislike. "The two parties had gone to law, and there had always been an ill-feeling between them" (189; *cf.* 371 col. 10).

那 *na*, THAT.

(83) This is occasionally used instead of the former in depositions when the very words which were or might have been used by a witness are as nearly as possible adhered to. We, therefore, find 那船, *na ch'uan* that vessel (6) and 那日 *na jih* on that day (179). In the first named example the witness supposed to have used the word *na*, is an English sailor whose deposition has to be translated by a witness;

it appears, therefrom, that these colloquialisms (*cf.* the 把我 *pa-wo* for "me" occurring in the same document) are peculiar to depositions in general. Otherwise they will hardly be met with in documents.

本 *pên*, THIS.

(84) This word may come to mean about as much as a demonstrative pronoun, though it has also a shade of the personal pronoun contained in it. We may frequently explain it as meaning "this my," "this our;" it is also used for 今 *chin*, "the present," and its translation varies in every particular case; with all its various meanings, most of which express some grammatical relation, it is almost a speciality of the business style.

The primary meaning being "root," "origin," it has become a prefix placed before nouns, in order to distinguish them as peculiar to the person of the writer, to the place where, and the time in which, he writes.

The person of the writer is alluded to by *pên* in official despatches when it precedes the writer's title. We may then consider it to take, *with* the title, the place of a personal pronoun,—whether of the first or third person, depends upon the style adopted in our translation. We may translate 經¹ 本² 大³ 臣⁴ 嚴⁵ 飭⁶ 放⁷ 行⁸ by ²*pên*-³*ta*-⁴*ch'ên* "I the minister ¹*ching* have," "*I have*;" or "the minister has,", "*he has*"—⁵*yen* strictly ⁶*ch'ih* ordered to ⁷*fang*-⁸*hsing* release (the ship) (11). It should be noted that of each official title there exists a certain contracted form which is, by etiquette and usage, invariably used in connection with 本 *pên*, the pronoun of the writer's person, as well as with 貴 *kuei*, the pronoun of the person of the addressee, as we should call it by way of analogy. This shorter form as it occurs in the context, usually consists of one or two characters only, whereas the name and full title of the writer with all its epithets occupies the first column on the right hand, either written by hand or impressed in black ink with a wooden stamp; that of the addressee, before the date and official seal at the end of the document.* The following examples show some of the contracted titles in common use, to which either *pên* or *kuei* is prefixed as the the case may be; on referring to Mayers' "The Chinese Government"†, the student will find the equivalent titles of about all the important posts in the Empire.

本大臣 *ta-ch'ên*, ministers of state, as also the foreign ministers and Imperial Commissioners.

本部堂 *pu-t'ang*, a Governor-General (in his capacity as an ex-officio President of the Board of War).

本部院 *pu-yüan*, a Provincial Governor.

本關部 *kuan-pu*, the Hoppo at Canton.

本　道 *tao*, a Tao-t'ai.

本　府 *fu*, a Prefect.

本　縣 *hsien*, a District Magistrate.

Beginners should take care to avoid confusion with regard to this particular point inasmuch as it is customary, when passages are quoted from other documents, to copy the word 本 *pên*, as it occurs in the original text. A complete Chinese despatch is to record the whole correspondence passed on the subject in question; in order to arrive at its contents, therefore, we have frequently to first unpack its accessories, as it were, like a set of Japanese boxes. It may, for instance, commence by saying: "Whereas *pên-tao* I, the Tao-t'ai, have been addressed by *kuei-fu*, you, the Prefect, who in

* This is the form adopted in despatches, proclamations, etc., issued by persons in office. In official and private notes, the writer's name is not mentioned, except on a card forming a separate inclosure, and on the face of the envelope; but the words 本 *pên* and 貴 *kuei* followed by short titles are also, though sparingly, used.

† "The Chinese Government; a Manual of Chinese Titles," etc. By W. F. Mayers. Second Edition, with Additions, by G. M. H. Playfair. Shanghai, 1886.

his despatch says, *pên-fu*, I, the Prefect, have received a letter from *kuei-hsien*, you, the Magistrate, who says *pên-hsien*, I, the Magistrate, have received a petition from three merchants A. B. and C. saying that *i-êtng*, "the ants," *i.e.* Petitioners, pray that, etc., whereupon *pên-hsien*, I, the Magistrate, forward the petition to *kuei-fu*, you, the Prefect, who again submits it to *kuei-tao*, you, the Tao-t'ai. Now, *pên-tao*, I, the Tao-t'ai, having received the foregoing, decide that, etc., which decision *kuei-fu*, you, the Prefect, are requested to forward to *kai hsien*, the said Magistrate, who is to communicate it to *kai shang*, the said merchants." In the case of despatches thus complicated one has to be careful to distinguish who is who by keeping in mind that the *pên* and *kuei* (as well as similar prefixes taking their place, like 弊 *pi*, standing for *pên*, as a term of modesty) with their respective titles are simply copied from the context of the despatches quoted.

(85) The place where the writer lives or to which he belongs is alluded to in expressions like 本署 *pên-shu*, "the court or yamên of which I am in charge," "this court"; 本館 *pên-kuan*, this office; 本行 *pên-hang*, this firm, this house; 本口 *pên-k'ou*, this port; 本國 *pên-kuo*, "the country to which I belong," "my native country;" 本地 *pên-ti*, this country, this place; hence 本地人 *pên-ti-jên*, natives of a place.

The time in which one writes is expressed in 本年 *pên-nien* (= 今年 *chin-nien*), the present year; this year (47); 本月 *pên-yüeh*, this month; 本朝 *pên-ch'ao*, during the present dynasty; this dynasty.

之 *chih* AS A PRONOUN.

(86) The use of this word as a pronoun whether personal or demonstrative is rare in the business style when compared to its use in the classical and mediæval language. As many

writers, however, like to introduce classical reminiscences, the remarks made by Julien in his "Monographie de *tchi* 之*,*" *Syntaxe Nouvelle*, Vol. I, p. 73 seqq., often help to explain difficulties in the documentary style. In the following sentences *chih* has undoubtedly a pronominal meaning.

土¹ 民² 一³ 人⁴ 犯⁵ 罪⁶ 土⁷ 司⁸ 縛⁹ 而¹⁰ 殺¹¹ 之¹² when ³; a ⁴*jên* man of the ¹*t'u* native ²*min* people ⁵*fan*-⁶*tsui* becomes guilty of a criminal offence, the ⁷*t'u*-⁸*ss* local rulers, T'u-ssŭ, will ⁹*fo* bind ¹⁰*êrh* and ¹¹*sha* kill ¹²*chih* HIM (309).

或¹ 與² 漢³ 民⁴ 有⁵ 唉⁶ 眦⁷ 輒⁸ 乘⁹ 夜¹⁰ 率¹¹ 衆¹² 環¹³ 北¹⁴ 屋¹⁵ 焚¹⁶ 而¹⁷ 屠¹⁸ 之¹⁹ [speaking of the aborigines in Yünnan] ¹*huo* if ²*yü* with ³*han*-⁴*min* the Chinese ⁶*yu* there is, they have ⁶*ai*-⁷*chai* angry glances, an ill-feeling ⁸*ch* then (marking the beginning of the main clause) ⁹*sh ng* taking advantage of ¹⁰*yeh* the night (they will) ¹¹*shuai*-¹²*chung* form bands, ¹³*huan* surround ¹⁴*ch'i* of them, their ¹⁵*wu* houses, ¹⁶*f n* burn them down ¹⁷*rh* and ¹⁸*t'u* kill ¹⁹*chih* THEM, *illos*. "If there happens to be an ill-feeling between the aborigines and the Chinese, the former will form bands at night, surround Chinese houses, burn them down and kill their inhabitants" (308).

但¹ 恐² 該³ 處⁴ 地⁵ 方⁶ 官⁷ 見⁸ 之⁹ 致¹⁰ 生¹¹ 疑¹² 惑¹³ ¹*tan* but ²*k'ung* we fear that if ⁵*ti*-⁶*fang*-⁷*kuan* the local authorities of ³*ka* ⁴*ch'u* the place ⁸*chien* see ⁹*chih* IT, it will ¹⁰*chih*-¹¹*shêng* create, result in ¹²*i*-¹³*huo* doubt, suspicion. "[The writers are quite sure that it was merely a slip of the pen that the name of the Interpreter Hsi Wei-lien was written Hsi Wei-ling;] *but as the difference might have made the authorities of the place he is about to visit suspicious* [they have thought it right to correct this also]" (51).

斯 *ssŭ*, THIS, THAT.

(87) As a demonstrative pronoun we have also to mention 斯 *ssŭ*. Its meaning is similar to that of 是 *shih*, this, that.

斯時 *ssŭ shih*, this time;
斯人 *ssŭ jĕn*, this man, this person;
斯事 *ssŭ shih*, this affair.

若 *jo*, THIS, SUCH.

(88)   This, otherwise conditional, particle is occasionally used as a demonstrative pronoun ("dans le sens de 此," Julien I, p. 225). 彼¹ 此² 判³ 若⁴ 兩⁵ 途¹ to ¹*pi-*²*tz'ŭ* here and there ³*p'an* distinguish, we may decide between ⁴*jo* these ⁵*liang* two ⁶*t'u* ways; "there are the following two methods of doing it, viz.," etc. (206).

若輩 *jo-pei*, of this sort or class, thus; 往¹ 往² 若³ 輩⁴ 爲⁵ 之⁶ ⁵*wei* they do ⁶*chih* it ¹*wang-*²*wang* frequently ³*jo-*⁴*pei* (= 如 此) like this; "it is often so" (266).

Reflexive Pronouns.

自 *tzŭ*, SELF.

(89)   Of this word compound forms may be used, as 自己 *tz-chi*, 自家 *tzŭ-chia*, 自身 *tzŭ-shên*, but the single word is more adapted to the written language, as in 自爲 *tzŭ wei*, self done, *i.e.* done by myself, yourself, etc.; 自新 *tzŭ-hsin* to renew one's self, to reform.

From the meaning *self* there is only a short step to that of the German "selbstverständlich," self-evident, *of course*. In this sense it is very commonly used in the despatch style, eg.

至¹ 匪² 徒³ 窺⁴ 伺⁵ 武⁶ 新⁷ 之⁸ 謠⁹ 自¹⁰ 屬¹¹ 無¹² 稽¹³—¹*chih as* to ⁹*yao* the rumour ⁸*chih* of ⁴*fei-*³*t'u* the out-laws ⁴*k'uei-*⁵*ssŭ* reconnoitering ⁶*wu* ⁷*hsin* the country of Wu and Hsin, ¹¹*shu* it is ¹⁰*tzŭ* of course ¹²*wu* not having, without ¹³*chi* proof. "As to the rumour that the out-laws were privily reconnoitering Wu-kang and Hsin-ning, it is no doubt groundless" (98).

查¹ 該² 員³ 等⁴ 所⁵ 禀⁶ 自⁷ 係⁸ 實⁹ 在¹⁰ 情¹¹ 形¹² 應¹³ 如¹⁴ 禀¹⁵ 辦¹⁶ 理¹⁷—¹ch'a considering that ⁵so that which ²kai the said ³yüan-⁴t'ing officers ⁶p'ing pray for ⁸hsi is ⁷tzŭ of course ⁹shih-¹⁰tsai the real ¹¹ch'ing-¹²hsing fact, [the matter] ¹³ying must be ¹⁶pan-¹⁷li managed ¹⁴ju as ¹⁵p'ing prayed for. "As the details put forward by those officers in their statement are no doubt correct, the petition is to be granted" (384; cf. 99 col. 3).

己 chi IPSE; SEMET IPSUM.

(90) The last named meaning attaches to chi in phrases like 肥 己 fei chi to fatten, to enrich one's self (350 col. 7; and 431 col. 1); 私 己 ssŭ chi to appropriate to one's self; 安 分 守 己 an-fên shou-chi, to mind one's own duties; 克 己 k'o-chi, to conquer one's self (Prémare). As stated above this word enters into composition with 自 tzŭ, e.g.

愿¹ 將² 自³ 己⁴ 洋⁵ 布⁶ 四⁷ 十⁸ 包⁹ 作¹⁰ 爲¹¹ 按¹² 當¹³—the writer ¹yüan wishes to ¹⁰tso-¹¹wei make ²chiang (sign of the object) ⁷ssŭ-⁸shih forty ⁹pao bales of ⁵yang-⁶pu Shirtings ³tzŭ-⁴chi of himself, being his property, ¹²an-¹³tang a pawn, a security (supplementary object). "He wished to pawn forty bales Shirtings, his property" (407).

親 ch'in IPSE.

(91) This word means that the action of a verb is done in person, or that the noun it may precede is in the most intimate personal connection with the subject.

此¹ 案² 着³ 交⁴ 韓⁵ 文⁶ 綺⁷ 親⁸ 提⁹ 人¹⁰ 證¹¹ 卷¹² 宗¹³— ¹tz'ŭ ²an this case ³cho I, the Emperor, command that; let ⁴chiao it be given to ⁵han-⁶wên-⁷ch'i Han Wên-ch'i to ⁹t'i have brought before him ⁸ch'in in person, i.e. brought before his person ¹⁰jên-¹¹chêng the witnesses and ¹²chüan-¹³tsung records of the case. "Let this case be handed over to Han Wên-ch'i, and let him have brought before him the necessary witness and paper" (188).

親¹ 手² 殺³ 人⁴,—³sha to kill ⁴jén a man ¹ch'in ipsâ ²shou manu, "with one's own hand."

親¹ 筆² 筆³ 之⁴—he ³pi wrote ⁴chih it ¹ch'in-²pi with his own pencil; "it is his hand writing" (Prémare).

RECIPROCAL PRONOUNS : 互 hu, 相 hsiang.

(92) The above two words, whether separate or combined, express mutuality, and may be generally translated by "each other" or "mutual."

該¹ 兵² 勇³ 等⁴ 互⁵ 歐⁶,—¹kai the, those ²ping regular soldiers and ³yung volunteers ⁴têng (sign of the plural) ⁶ou fight ⁵hu with each other, "there was a collision between the regulars and the volunteers" (100).

將¹ 所² 奉³ 欽⁴ 賜⁵ 之⁶ 權⁷. 互⁸ 相⁹ 較¹⁰ 閱¹¹—To ⁸hu-⁹hsiang mutually ¹⁰chiao-¹¹yüeh examine ¹chiang (sign of the object) the ⁷ch'üan authorities, full powers ²so...⁶chih which ⁸fêng were received as ⁴ch'in-tz'ǎ granted by the monarch (American Treaty).

互 結 hu chieh, a mutual agreement (77 col. 10).

互 相 呈 控 hu-hsiang ch'êng-k'ung, they accuse each other (35).

相 對 hsiang tui, to mutually agree, to tally with each other.

相 同 hsiang t'ung, each the same as the other (Wade, Note 29 to Paper 1).

In phrases like 相應 hsiang-ying, 相當 hsiang-tang, etc., it is one's duty to another, "as in duty bound," the relation expressed between two persons need not be mutual. 相應照會 hsiang-ying chao-hui means "I send a despatch as it is my official duty to do so" (cf. 5 col. 1, with Note 28 to Paper 2).

RELATIVE PRONOUNS.

(93) The use of these pronouns is much more economical in Chinese than it is in Western languages, relative sentences

being very frequently expressed by mere anteposition with or without 之 *chih*, as shewn in the chapter treating upon the genitive case in its various phases. The relative pronoun used in connection with this construction, it has been stated there, is 所 *so*. The force of a relative clause is also expressed by the substitution of a participial phrase with *ché* 者, which may be modified by being preceded by 凡 *fan*= quisquis, quicunque; but apart from these, there is only one word which may be called a relative pronoun, namely 攸 *yu*.

所 *so* : QUI, QUÆ, QUOD.

(94) It has been shewn that, to understand the construction of an ordinary relative clause in Chinese, we should assume that all that is said in it, precedes the noun of which it is dependent as a genitive, with or without 之; that 所 *so* may be added without altering the general construction, and that it is placed after the subject, but before the verb, of the clause (*see* paragr. 48 on p. 57).

This rule refers to ordinary cases in which the relative clause is made dependent upon a noun. The construction with 所 *so*, however, also expresses relations not coming within this class of sentences, and which should, therefore, be treated as exceptional, *viz.*

1st. Without referring to any noun at all, the relative clause may come to represent a noun itself; its meaning is, then, that of a participial phrase. In this case, 所 *so*, standing after the subject (if mentioned) and before the verb of the clause, cannot be left out; it may in these examples be said to correspond to the Latin *is qui, id quod,* etc.

其[1] 所[2] 欲[3]—[2]*so* id quod [1]*ch'i* ille (subject) [3]*yü* desiderat (verb), "that which he desires," "his desires."

凡[1] 其[2] 所[3] 有[4]—[1]*fan*-[3]*so* all that which *ch'i* he [4]*yu* has, "whatsoever he has,"—"all his property."

視¹ 其² 所³ 以⁴ 觀⁵ 其⁶ 所⁷ 由⁸—¹*shih* look to ³*so* that which ²*ch'i* he ⁴*i* uses, ⁵*uan* behold ⁷*so* that which ⁶*ch'i* he ⁸*yu* is guided by, the principles from which he acts (*Lun-yü*).

上¹ 諭² 各³ 督⁴ 撫⁵ 嚴⁶ 飭⁷ 所⁸ 屬⁹,—¹*shang-*²*yü* an imperial edict commands ³*ko-*⁴*tu-*⁵*fu* the governors general and governors to ⁶*yen* strictly ⁷*ch'ih* order ⁸*so* those who ⁹*shu* belong to their resort, etc. (236 col. 2 ; *cf. ibid.* col. 4).

2nd. Instead of referring to a noun following, the relative clause may be dependent upon a word preceding it, and this word may not even be a noun, though the sense of a noun must be implied in it such as 無 *wu*, there is not anything, there is nothing,* or 何 '*ho*, what is there ? The subject of the clause, as the following examples show, may be implied in its verb.

無¹ 所² 不³ 為⁴—¹*wu* there is not anything ²*so* which ⁴*wei* he does ³*pu* not; " there is nothing that he does not do," *i.e.* " he does everything." The noun upon which the relative clause depends is here implied in *wu* 無 ; the subject of the clause itself, " he," is contained in the verb *wei* 為.

無¹ 所² 不³ 能⁴—¹*wu* there is nothing ²*so* which ³*pu* ⁴*néng* he is not able (to do), *i.e.* " he is omnipotent."

何¹ 所² 不³ 至⁴—¹*ho* what is there ²*so* that ³*pu-*⁴*chih* he does not reach ? " where does he not go to ?" *i.e.* " he goes everywhere, is omnipresent, universal."

何¹ 所² 不³ 顧⁴—¹*ho* what is there ²*so* that ³*pu-*⁴*ku* he does not attend to ? *i.e.* " he attends to everything."

3rd. The relative pronoun 所 *so* is sometimes used to make a certain inverted construction more intelligible, when the subject of a phrase is to be emphasized, as if we were to say: " it was not *me* who did it," instead of using the simpler form : " *I* did not do it." In such cases the logical object

* The Chinese glossator consulted by Julien in his "Table des Idiotismes," p. 281, Vol. 1 of the *Syntaxe nouvelle*, explains it by 無一件 *wu-i-chien*.

may appear at the head of the sentence, followed by (1) the subject, (2) 所 *so*, and (3) the verb in the order just mentioned. Such inversions will be still better understood if we explain the verb as being in the passive voice and the noun preceding 所 *so* as the doer of the action which in Latin would be introduced by *a cum ablativo*.

鬧¹ 事² 斷³ 非⁴ 我⁵ 輩⁶ 所⁷ 爲⁸—¹*nao* ²*shih* the trouble (it is) ³*tuan*-⁴*fei* not at all, by no means ⁵*wo*-⁶*pei* we ⁷*so* who ⁸*wei* did it; or, giving the verb passive construction: "the trouble was certainly not done by us" (325).

爲¹ 婦² 人³ 所⁴ 惑⁵—¹*wei* it was ²*fu*-³*j'n* his wife ⁴*so* that ⁵*huo* led him astray, or "he was led astray by his wife."

照¹ 得² 穀³ 米⁴ 爲⁵ 民⁶ 食⁷ 所⁸ 關⁹—¹*chao*-²*tê* whereas ⁵*wei* it is ⁶*min*-⁷*shih* the people's food ⁸*so* which ⁹*kuan* is related to, is concerned in ³*ku*-⁴*mi* grain. "Whereas grain is an article concerned in the maintenance of the people" (430).

知¹ 何² 員³ 所⁴ 查⁵—¹*chih* to know ²*ho* what ³*yüan* officer [it is] ⁴*so* who ⁵*ch'a* made the examination, "to know who has been the examining officer" (268).

(95)   The phrase 所以 *so-i*, usually translated by "whence," or "therefore," must be considered as a sort of relative clause; it is, indeed, the relative form corresponding to the demonstrative 是 以 *shih-i* and has often the same meaning (*cf.* Julien: "ce par quoi, ce pourquoi," Vol. I p. 97).

除¹ 害² 卽³ 所⁴ 以⁵ 興⁶ 利⁷ 也⁸—[if we] ¹*ch'u* remove ²*hai* the injurious influences, ³*chi* then [there will be] ⁴*so*-⁵*i* that by which ⁶*hsing*-⁷*li* we shall give rise to profit ⁸*yeh* (final particle). "To furnish the means to prosperity by arresting mischief" (124).

爲¹ 民² 卽³ 所⁴ 以⁵ 爲⁶ 已⁷—[if we] ¹*wei* act for ²*min* the people ³*chi* then [we have] ⁴*so*-⁵*i* that by which, whereby, ⁶*wei* to act for ⁷*chi* ourselves; "serving the people you serve yourselves" (108).

此¹ 無² 本³ 之⁴ 礦⁵ 民⁶ 所⁷ 以⁸ 困⁹ 也¹⁰—¹tz'ǔ this is ⁷so-⁸i that by which ⁵kung-⁶min the mining people ⁴chih who ²wu have no ³pên capital ⁹k'un get impoverished ¹⁰yeh (final particle). "This is the reason why the miners who work without capital are reduced to poverty" (348).

(96) 以 i has by itself relative force originally even in such cases where, as in the maxims of the Sacred Edict, we choose to translate it by "*in order to.*" In the following example it may be said to stand for 所以 so-i.

濟¹ 貧² 卽³ 以⁴ 安⁵ 富⁶—[if we] ¹chi assist ²pin the poor ³chi then [that will be] ⁴i that by which [we may] ⁵an make easy ⁶fu the rich. "Relief of the poor is a means to the security of the wealthy" (116).

(97) The phrase 所有 so-yu, also originally coming within this category, has been discussed in paragr. 14 on p. 32.

攸 yu: QUI, QUAE, QUOD.

(98) This pronoun has very much the same meaning as 所 so and is similarly applied.

事¹ 爲² 衆³ 食⁴ 攸⁵ 關⁶—²wei it is ³chung-⁴shih the food of the masses, the people ⁵yu which ⁶kuan is related to, is concerned in ¹shih the matter. "The matter concerns, has to do with, the maintenance of the people" (431; *cf.* the example quoted in paragr. 94 from p. 430, where 所 so is used in a similar context).

者 chê.

(99) This character following a verb or a sentence gives it participial force (if not the force of a noun), or that of a relative clause, inasmuch as we may choose either the one or the other in translating. If translated by a relative pronoun it corresponds to Latin "is qui," etc.

刼¹ 財² 者³ 稱⁴ 爲⁵ 强⁶ 盜⁷—³chê those who ¹chieh carry off ²ts'ai property ⁴ch'êng-⁵wei are called ⁶ch'iang-⁷tao robbers (416).

例¹ 前² 入³ 洋⁴ 者⁵ 勒⁶ 限⁷ 三⁸ 年⁹ 回¹⁰ 籍¹¹ 例¹² 後¹³ 入¹⁴
洋¹⁵ 者¹⁶ 不¹⁷ 准¹⁸ 回¹⁹ 籍²⁰,—⁵chě those who ³ju-⁴yang have
entered the ocean, *i.e.* have emigrated ²ch'ien previous to ¹li
the law [regulating emigration] ⁶lê are bound ⁷hsien limiting
⁸san ⁹nien three years ¹⁰hui-¹¹chi to return to their home
¹⁶chě those who ¹⁴ju-¹⁵yang have emigrated ¹²li-¹³hou after
the law ¹⁷pu-¹⁸chun are not permitted to ¹⁹hui-²⁰chi return.

"Emigrants who left China previous to the emigration law
being put in force must return to their home within three
years' limit; emigrants who left afterwards are forbidden
to return" (128; *cf.* 345 col. 11; 416 col. 7; 430 col. 12 seq).

(100)   This construction with 者 *chě*, whether looked upon
as representing a relative clause, or a participial expression,
or a noun, is very frequently preceded by a sort of apposition,
or a genitive by position as we may fitly explain it: "of the
so and so those who, etc."

子¹ 毆² 父³ 母⁴ 殺⁵ 者⁶ 淩⁷ 遲⁸ 處⁹ 死¹⁰—¹tzŭ of children
(genitive by position) ⁶chě those who, ²ou striking ³fu-⁴mu
father or mother, ⁵sha kill ⁹ch'u-¹⁰ssŭ are punished by the
death of ⁷ling-⁸ch'ih being cut to pieces, or "children who
strike their parents to death are punished by death through
the process of being cut to pieces" (202).

天¹ 下² 銅³ 斤⁴ 產⁵ 於⁶ 滇⁷ 者⁸ 十⁹ 之¹⁰ 五¹¹ 六¹² 產¹³ 他¹⁴
省¹⁵ 者¹⁶ 十¹⁷ 之¹⁸ 三¹⁹ 四²⁰—¹t'ien-²hsia ³t'ung-⁴chin of the
world's copper, of all the copper produced in the Empire
[genitive by position], ⁸chě that which ⁵ch'an is produced
⁶yü in ⁷tien Yünnan [is, makes, constitutes] ¹¹wu ¹²liu five
or six [parts] ¹⁰chih of, out of ⁹shih ten; ¹⁶chě that which
¹³ch'an is produced in ¹⁴t'a other ¹⁵shěng provinces, ¹⁹san
²⁰ssŭ three or four [parts] ¹⁸chih out of ¹⁷shih ten. "Yünnan
furnishes five or six tenths, other provinces three or four
tenths, of all the copper produced in China" (347; *cf.* 331
col. 3; 352 col. 8; 261 col. 1 seqq.; 264 col. 6 seq.).

嗣¹ 後² 有³ 案⁴ 情⁵ 似⁶ 此⁷ 者⁸—if ¹ssŭ-²hou hereafter ³yu there are ⁴an-⁵ching of circumstances ⁸chê those which, such which ⁶ssï resemble ⁷tz'ï these. "From this time forth, in all cases in which the circumstances resemble these," etc. (202).

The construction with 其 ch'i.. and 者 chê, may be similarly explained. In this case the literal translation of the phrase is "of these those who." Cf. the examples under 其 ch'i paragr. 77 p. 75.

(101)　A relative clause with 者 chê may be headed by the indefinite pronoun 凡 fan. In this case the two pronouns together produce the sense of the Latin quisquis.

凡¹ 爲² 地³ 方⁴ 官⁵ 者⁶—¹fan…⁶chê all those who ²wei are, act as ³ti-⁴fang-⁵kuan local authorities.

凡¹ 有² 益³ 於⁴ 疏⁵ 銷⁶ 者⁷—¹fan..⁷chê all those who ²yu have ³i advantage ⁴yü in ⁵su-⁶hsiao free circulation.

The Ta-ch'ing lü-li or Chinese Penal Code abounds with examples of this class. It should be noted that 凡 fan, meaning "whoever," also "whenever," may be employed without 者 chê (3 col. 6).

(102)　As with 凡 fan, the word 者 chê may also be combined with 所 so and 所以 so-i.

今¹ 所² 積³ 壓⁴ 者⁵—²so..⁵chê those which have ¹chin now ³chi-⁴ya accumulated (354 col. 7).

(103)　The particle 者 chê added to a verb or a verbal expression gives it the force of a noun.

爲¹ 難² 者³,—³chê that which ¹wei makes ²nan difficulties, i.e. the making of difficulties, difficulties (374 col. 10).

〇〇〇其¹ 難² 辦³ 者⁴ 一⁵ 也⁶……⁶yeh is ¹ch'i of it ⁵i the first ²nan-³pan-⁴chê difficulty in managing. "This is the first difficult point in the matter" (352; cf. 353 col. 2; 354 col. 1).

目¹ 今² 開³ 洋⁴ 採⁵ 買⁶ 而⁷ 銅⁸ 斤⁹ 反¹⁰ 致¹¹ 缺¹² 額¹³ 者¹⁴

以^{15}滇^{16}銅^{17}不^{18}出^{19}故^{20}也^{21}—^{14}ché, here corresponding to the Greek τὸ before an infinitive, translate: "the fact that" ^{1}mu-^{2}chin now ^{3}k'ai-^{4}yang we have opened the ocean i.e. allowed foreign trade and ^{5}ts'ai-^{6}mai purchase [copper from other countries] ^{7}êrh ^{10}fan and that yet ^{8}t'ung-^{9}chin the quantity of copper ^{11}chih has come to ^{12}ch'üeh-^{13}ngo a deficit ^{19}i ^{20}ku is caused by ^{16}tien-^{17}t'ung Yünnan copper ^{18}pu-^{19}ch'u not being exported ^{21}yeh (final particle). "The reason for a deficit having appeared in the supply of copper in spite of importation from other countries being free is, that no copper has been exported from Yünnan" (347).

以^{1}足^{2}民^{3}者^{4}裕^{5}國^6—^{5}yü to benefit ^{6}kuo the state ^{1}i by ^{2}tsu ^{3}min ^{4}ché satisfying the people, supplying the wants of the people (319).

(104). We may here mention phrases like 啓者 ch'i-ché, "a communication," "an advice," from the verb 啓 ch'i to inform (47 col. 9; etc.), 敬啓者 ching ch'i-ché, "a respectful communication," 敬覆者 ching fu-ché, "a respectful reply;" 敬稟者 ching ping-ché, "a respectful petition" (104 col. 9; 391 col. 9), which are used as headings as it were in letters and petitions respectively; also the phrase concluding official despatches exchanged between foreign and Chinese officials: 須^{1}至^{2}照^{3}會^{4}者^5 ^{3}chao-^{4}hui ^{5}ché a despatch [^{5}chi giving the verb ^{3}chao-^{4}hui="to address officially," the force of a noun] ^{1}hsü ^{2}chih that must go and arrive, i.e. "a necessary despatch," as it is usually translated; or as Chinese writers say between themselves 須^{1}至^{2}移^{3}者^4 ^{3}i-^{4}ché a communication [^{4}ché giving the verb ^{3}i="to communicate officially," the force of a noun] ^{1}hsü ^{2}chih that must go and arrive, i.e. "a necessary communication" (99 col. 12; 102 col. 5).

(105) When following a noun 者 ché gives it the force of an *adjective* with the article e.g. 德者 té-ché the virtuous,

from 德 tê, virtue; 仁者 jên-chê, the humane, from 仁 jên, humanity; 病者 ping-chê, the patient, from 病 ping sickness (47 col. 2).

(106) In explanations and definitions 者 chê is appended to the term to be defined, whereas the characters forming the explanation are followed by 也 yeh, here representing the substantive verb "to be." 德^1 者^2 本^3 也^4,—^{1}tê-^{2}chê virtue ^{4}yeh that is ^{3}pên the root. (Prémare, p. 184). This is the standard form of definitions as used in Dictionaries. But 也 yeh is not essential (cf. Prémare II, 2, 4) as the following example shows.

夫^1 銅^2 斤^3 者^4 錢^5 法^6 之^7 源^8 錢^9 法^{10} 者^{11} 銅^{12} 斤^{13} 之^{14} 流^{15}—^{1}fu, a prefix (considered part of the construction in connexion with ^{4}chê by Prémare, 1, 2, 3) ^{2}t'ung-^{3}chin ^{4}chê copper, that is ^{8}yüan the source ^{7}chih of ^{5}ch'ien-^{6}fa coinage; ^{9}ch'ien-^{10}fa ^{11}chê, coinage, that is ^{15}liu the flowing, the circulation ^{14}chih of ^{12}t'ung-^{13}chin copper. "As copper is the basis for coining cash, cash is again the means of circulation for copper" (350).

(107) 者 chê is added to certain adverbs without changing their meaning, as 昔者 hsi-chê, formerly; 茲者 tzŭ-chê, now (58 col. 8); 今者 chin-chê, now; 再者 tsai-chê, further, again (used at the beginning of a new subject or of a postscript (Williams; 412 col. 3); 一者 i-chê, once, this time only (Williams).

DISTRIBUTIVE PRONOUNS.

(108) As such we may consider 各 ko and 每 mei both meaning "each, every." The former may be frequently translated by the plural of the noun following, especially when preceded by an adjective or a genitive; without such an attribute 各 ko will be generally found to retain its pronominal force as each, every, all, e.g. 各國 ko-kuo, every nation, all nations; in a limited sense, the nations having concluded

treaties with China, *i.e.* all the treaty powers; 各 項 *ko hsiang*, every kind, all kinds; 各 色 *ko sĕ*, every description, all descriptions; 各 辦 各 事 *ko pan ko shih*, every one managing his own business. 各 *ko* has rather a tendency to express totality whereas 每 *mei* is a purely distributive pronoun; 每 人 *mei jén* every man, every single man; 每 一 件 事 *mei i-chien shih*, every affair. In phrases like 每 時 *mei shih*, each time, *mei* may be separated from its noun by a genitive as we have seen already, or precede the whole phrase as an adverbial expression, *e.g.*

每¹ 於² 對³ 仗⁴ 之⁵ 時⁶—¹*mei* each time, always ²*yü* at ⁶*shih* the time ⁵*chih* of ³*tui*-⁴*chang* fighting, *i.e.* "WHENEVER · fighting takes place" (397; *cf.* 248 col. 11).

INDEFINITE PRONOUNS: 某, *mou*, QUIDAM.

(109) If the writer does not wish or is not able to mention the name of a person, *i.e.* if we would use the pronoun *quidam* in Latin, or say "a certain [*i.e.* an uncertain] so and so," the Chinese commonly employ the character 某 *mou*, as in 某 人 *mou jén*, a certain person; 某 客 *mou k'o*, a certain stranger; 老 母 某 氏 *lao-mu mou-shih*, an old mother of such and such a name; here *mou* takes the place of a female name, and is followed by *shih* just as if the name were mentioned; we may say "old Mrs. So and So." In *pro formâ* copies of forms or in other documents, when names are omitted, the space which would otherwise be occupied by a name may be filled up by 某 某 *mou mou* (407 col. 6; 411 col. 3); or 某 人 *mou jén* (see Papers 55 and 56); dates left blank for some reason or other may be filled up by the same word as in 某 年 某 月 *mou-nien mou-yüeh*, "in such and such a month of such and such a year," or "in the...month of the...year" (407 col. 10).

同 *t'ung* THE SAME; 異 *i*, NOT THE SAME, DIFFERENT.

(110) 同 *t'ung* and 異 *i* are opposites; the negation of the

one involves the position of the other, *i.e.* 不同 *pu-tʻung*= 異 *i*; and 不異 *pu-i* or 無異 *wu-i*=同 *tʻung*.

The words "as" after "the same," and "from" after "different," are expressed by the preposition 與 *yü* as has been shewn on a previous occasion.

與¹ 該² 弁³ 等⁴ 所⁵ 稟⁶ 畧⁷ 同⁸—⁷*lio* on the whole ⁸*tʻung* the same ¹*yü* AS ⁵*so* that which ²*kai* the said ³*pien-*⁴*tĕng* officers ⁶*ping* state (394 col. 11 ; *cf. ibid.* col. 9).

與¹ 瓦² 民³ 無⁴ 異⁵—⁴*wu-*⁵*i* not different ¹*yü* from ²*liang* good ³*min* people, subjects (308).

(111) 與 *yü* always precedes 異 *i* or 同 *tʻung* with the term of comparison; there is, however, yet another construction in which 異 *i*, different, is followed by the object compared, though with another preposition, *viz.*, 於 *yü*, here corresponding to the Latin *quam*, *e.g.*

異¹ 於² 常³ 年⁴—¹*i*, different ²*yü* from (*i.e.* not the same as) ³*chʻang* ordinary ⁴*nien* years (122). *See* paragr. 60, p. 66.

(112) The omission of the preposition is very rare. As exceptional we may consider the phrase 同上 *tʻung-shang*, "the same AS the above," which is commonly used like our *ib.* or *ibid.* (=*ibidem*) in connection with quotations, meaning that a passage has been taken from the same source as the preceding quotation.

(113) 同 *tʻung* may be inforced by 相 *hsiang* (394 col.; 9' it also enters into composition with certain nouns in terms the meaning of which implies sameness in their being applied to several individuals, *e.g.* 同姓 *tʻung-hsing*, of the same surname. 同姓不同宗 *tʻung-hsing pu tʻung-tsung*, said of people having the same surname, but not being relations; 同年 *tʻung-nien*, of the same age; 同心一意 *tʻung-hsin-i-i* of the same opinion, etc.

—, *i*, ONE, EXPRESSING SAMENESS.

(114) From the last mentioned example it may be seen

how this character comes to be a synonym of 同 *t'ung*. — 意 *i-i*, one opinion, if held by two or more individuals, must, necessarily be the *same* opinion. Thus we may translate — 般 *i-pan*, lit. one manner, by "the same manner," — 面, *i-mien*, lit. one face, one looking at, by "at the same time," *e.g.* one statement (Morrison).

由¹ 縣² 發³ 給⁴ 腰⁵ 牌⁵ 護⁷ 照⁸ 一⁹ 面¹⁰ 示¹¹ 諭¹² 本¹³ 地¹⁴ 壯¹⁵ 丁¹⁶ 如¹⁷ 無¹⁸ 腰¹⁹ 牌²⁰ 印²¹ 照²² 不²³ 得²⁴ 擅²⁵ 自²⁶ 成²⁷ 羣²⁸ 結²⁹ 隊³⁰— ¹*yu* (sign of the subject) ²*hsien* the District Magistrate ³*fa*-⁴*chi* will issue ⁵*yao*-⁶*p'ai*-⁷*hu*-⁸*chao* belt-tickets and pass-ports and ⁹*i*-¹⁰*mien* at the same time ¹¹*shih*-¹²*yü* enjoin upon the ¹³*pĕn*-¹⁴*ti* native ¹⁵*chuang*-¹⁶*ting* volunteers (that) ¹⁷*ju* if ¹⁸*wu* not having, without ¹⁹*yao*-²⁰*p'ai* a belt ticket and ²¹*yin*-²²*chao* sealed pass-port, ²³*pu*-²⁴*tĕ* they must not ²⁵*shan*-²⁶*tzŭ* on their own authority ²⁷*ch'ĕng*-²⁸*ch'ün* form crowds and ²⁹*chieh*-³⁰*tui* band together.

"A belt-ticket and passport will then be issued to him by the District Magistrate, who is at the same time to notify to the volunteers of this Prefecture, that, if without a belt-ticket or sealed pass, they are not to take on them to form into gangs large or small" (103).

(115) Sameness of time is expressed in certain constructions formed with — *i*.

一¹ 聽² 即³ 答⁴—¹*i* once ²*t'ing* hear, (he) ³*chi* at once ⁴*ta* replied, *i.e.* he replied as soon as he heard (Williams).

一¹ 經² 拏³ 獲⁴ 即⁵ 行⁶ 從⁷ 重⁸ 究⁹ 治¹⁰—¹*i* as soon as (the offenders) ²*ching* (sign of the past) have been ³*na*-⁴*hu* seized ⁵*chi* then, at once (they must be) ⁶*hsing* (denoting the action of the following phrase) ⁷*ts'ung*-⁸*chung* severely *chiu-chih* tried (250).

(116) In examples of this class, — *i*, in its capacity of expressing sameness, assists in the construction of a temporal clause expressing simultaneousness of action. Its particular

force, as described in paragr. 5 on p. 22, in the adverbial phrases 一 體 *i-t'i*, 一 切 *i-ch'ieh*, 一 律 *i-lü*, 一 併 *i-ping* 一 概 *i-kai*, 一 同 *i-t'ung*, 一 齊, *i-ch'i*, etc., may also be derived from this general meaning of "sameness." The term 畫 一 *hua-i*, *lit.* oneness, or sameness, of drawing, *i.e.* uniformity, has a slight shade of it in the example ○○○以¹ 符² 稅³ 則¹ 而⁵ 昭³ 畫⁷ 一⁸, ¹*i* in order to ²*fu* accord with ³*shui*-⁴*tsê* the tariff ⁵*êrh* and ⁶*chao* make manifest ⁷*hua*-⁸*i* uniformity.

"....; such a course being in harmony with the Tariff, and one which gives a rule to be uniformly adhered to" (12; *cf*. 386 col. 12).

他 *t'a*, ALIUS.

(117) This word, used as a pronoun of the third person in the Mandarin colloquial, has the meaning *other*, *another*, in the written language, *e.g.* 他 省 *t'a-shêng*, other provinces; 他 日 *t'a-jih*, another day; 他 人 *t'a-jên*, another man. 他 言 *t'a-yen*, other words, 他 議 *t'a-i*, other schemes, and similar phrases, may be used with an *arrière pensée* of insincerity, easily explained by the contrast in the example quoted in K'ang-hsi's Dictionary:

君¹ 子² 正³ 而⁴ 不⁵ 他⁶—¹*chün*-²*tzŭ* the superior man is ³*chêng* upright ⁴*êrh* and ⁵*pu* not ⁶*t'a* otherwise, *i.e.* insincere, false.

INTERROGATIVE PRONOUNS.

(118) As we shall have to come back to these pronouns when speaking of interrogative sentences, it will be sufficient to here give a list of the principal pronouns of this class used in the business style with their respective meanings. They are

孰 *shu*, who? what?
誰 *shui*, who?
何 *ho* and 曷 *ho*, what?

These are about the only words corresponding to the Latin *quis, quid,* however rich the language is in interrogative particles serving to form interrogative sentences generally.

NUMERALS.

(119) The number of numeral characters used in the documentary style is thirteen; they consist of the numbers one to nine and certain signs expressing the successive decimals from ten to ten thousand (10, 100, 1000 and 10,000). The dictionary contains also characters for 100,000, a million, ten millions, and a hundred millions, but these are not used, as a rule, in forming higher numbers, the character for "ten thousand" being the highest factor employed in compound numbers. A million is thus expressed by " a hundred ten thousands," ten millions by "a thousand ten thousands," etc.

(120) Similiarly as we, in writing numbers, are at liberty to use the Arabic style (figures), or the Roman style (numbers), or to write them out in words, as may be required on special occasions, the Chinese have three modes of writing numbers, viz., the 原本 *yüan-p'ǹ, i.e.* the original or simple numerals; the 大寫 *ta-hsich, i.e.* the large style ; and the 花碼 *hua-ma,* the "flowery weight" or abbreviated style. Original numerals are those common in books, in ordinary accounts, reports, etc., if no special reason demands a different style. The *Ta-hsich,* on the other hand, corresponds to our numbers written in words and is similarly employed, *viz.* in all important documents such as accounts and reports to the government, on cheques and drafts, commercial bills, and generally wherever it is of importance to make sure that no fraudulent changes can be made in the writing. The character 二 *êrh,* two, as ordinarily written, for instance could be changed into 三 *san,* three, by the addition of a single stroke. In order to render such unauthorised changes more difficult, the *Ta-hsieh* style has been made to consist in

DOCUMENTARY STYLE.   99

a selection of characters sufficiently complicated to enable any addition to be at once discovered. This in connection with the fact that all Chinese paper will easily show any erasure made on it when held against the light, is certainly the best guaranty against fraud that could have been devised under the circumstances. The third, or abbreviated, form is a kind of running hand, the ordinary numeral characters having been reduced to the greatest simplicity imaginable. They are also called 蘇州碼數 *Su-chou ma-shu*, *i.e.* Su-chou numbers, on a supposition, perhaps, that their use has originated at Su-chou, the great city near Shanghai, though the fact of their being written from the left to the right hand, for which in the eyes of a Chinaman there seems to be no reasonable cause, the similarity of some of these signs to the corresponding Indian figures and the use of zeroes, have been taken as traces of western origin. These numeral short-hand signs are rarely seen in printed books, but are confined to ordinary account books, bills, memoes, etc.

(121)   The following is a list of the thirteen numeral characters as written in each of the three styles:

Yüan-pên.	Ta-hsieh.	Hua-ma.	
一	壹	丨	$i = 1.$
二	貳	丨丨	$êrh = 2.$
三	叁	丨丨丨	$san = 3.$
四	肆	ㄨ	$ssŭ = 4.$
五	伍	〇	$wu = 5.$
六	陸	亠	$liu = 6.$
七	柒	丄	$ch'i = 7.$
八	捌	丄丨	$pa = 8.$
九	玖	夊	$chiu = 9.$
十	拾	十	$shih = 10.$
百	佰	百	$pai = 100.$
千	仟	千	$ch'ien = 1000.$
萬	萬	万	$wan = 10,000.$

二十 *érh-shih*, twenty, is sometimes contracted to 廿 or 卄 (392 col. 2) *ju* (a double 十 *shih* ten) which form is again occasionally represented by 念 *nien*, said to be of local use at Shanghai by Williams p. 635 ; and 三十 *san-shih*, thirty, is similarly contracted to 卅 *sa;* but such abbreviated forms would not be admissible in strictly official writings.

(122) The character for 100,000 contained in the Dictionaries is 億 *i*, that for a million 兆 *chao*, that for ten millions 京 *ching*, and that for a hundred millions 垓 *kai*.* These signs, though not employed as factors in expressing high numbers in a definite sense, may occur in general phrases as 億¹ 兆² 之³ 衆⁴ ⁴*chung* a multitude ³*chih* of ¹*i* a hundred thousand ²*chao* millions, *i.e.* an innumerable mass of people; 兆民 *chao-min*, a million people, the million.

(123) It will be seen from the above table that since there was no need for it no separate character exists for the *Ta-hsieh* style of the decimal number 100,000.

(124) As regards the *Hua-ma* it should be noted that the signs ｜, ‖ and ⦀ are written horizontally, *viz*., -, = and ☰, when following any of those signs written vertically so as to avoid confusion, as in ├=12, ‖三| =231. The decimal may be written underneath the numeral occupying the highest decimal place in the number; and similarly the character standing for *tael, mace, candareen*, or *cash* is added below when necessary for the sake of clearness. Interruptions in the series are expressed by the insertion of zeroes, but no zeroes need be written at the end of a number as we would in numbers like 2,300, or 15,000. When numeral characters or money designations are added underneath the ordinary

---

* K'ang-hsi's Dictionary, Rad. 土 p. 11: 十¹ 億² 曰³ 兆⁴ 十⁵ 兆⁶ 曰⁷ 京⁸ 十⁹ 京¹⁰ 曰¹¹ 垓¹², *i.e.* ten ²*i* are called ⁴*chao*; ten ⁴*chao* are called ⁸*ching*; ten ⁸*ching* are called ¹²*kai*. Under 億 *i*, the Imperial Dictionary says that it means 十萬 *shih-wan,i.e.* ten times ten thousand, but that according to some its number is indefinite.

DOCUMENTARY STYLE. 101

figures, they usually assume the contracted shape as follows:

萬 wan = 万.
兩 liang = 双.
錢 ch'ien = 𨤾 (entering into various combinations with its number, as shown in the subjoined examples).
分 fên = 今.
厘 li = 乇.

千 ch'ien, 百 pai, and 十 shih do not differ from their ordinary shape except by appearing in diminished size.

EXAMPLES.

１㇆ = 65; １㇆㇄㇆ = Tls. 65.8.5.1
十   十双

Ⅲ㇆㇄ = 357; Ⅲ㇆㇄O㇆ = Tls. 357.0.5.1.
百   百双

Ⅲ㇄十 = 380; Ⅲ㇄OOO! = Tls. 380.0.0.1.
百   百   乇

ⅢO㇄ = 308; ⅢO㇄OO! = Tls. 308.0.0.1.
百   百   乇

Ⅱ㇆O㇈ = 2,509; Ⅱ㇆O㇈𨤾 = Tls. 2,509.4.0.0.
千   千

１㇄ = 68; １㇄㇆Ⅲ- = Tls. 68.5.3.1.
十   十双

１㇄十 = 680; １㇄O𨤾 = Tls. 680.3.0.0.
百   百

１㇄百 = 6,800; １㇄OO𨤾 = Tls. 6,800.1.0.0.
千   千

１O㇄十 = 6,080; １O㇄O𨤾 = Tls. 6,080.5.0.0.
千   千

１OO㇄ = 6,008; １OO㇄𨤾 = Tls. 6,008.6.00.
千   千

㇆ⅡOⅢ㇄ = 52,037; ㇆ⅡOⅢ㇄𨤾 = Tls. 52,037.7.0.0.
万   万

１O㇆㇈Ⅱ = 60,592; １O㇆㇈Ⅱ𨤾 = Tls. 60,592.8.0.0.
万   万

１Ⅱ = 62,000; ⅢOOO𨤾 = Tls. 62,000.9.0.0.
万   万

Ⅲ=Ⅱ㇆Ⅲ = 322,563.
十万

１=Ⅱ=Ⅱ-= 123,321.
十万

１ⅢO１㇆O㇄ = 6,306,508.
百十万

上州别一 = 63,521,000.

千百万
1别=0别州文 = Tls. 153,205,729.
万　十万　万

(125) The different decimals follow each other from the higher to the lower order. The numerals one to nine at the end of numbers are sometimes added with 有 yu, as in 十¹ 有² 五³ ¹shih ten ²yu having, with ³wu five i.e. fifteen (Cf. Julien, p. 198). 有 yu should in such cases be pronounced in the ch'ü-shêng, as it is explained as meaning 又 yu, "and."

(126) An interruption in the decimal series may be expressed by the character 零 ling which indeed "is used in any place but the last in a series of numbers in which we should insert zero" ("Wade, Colloquial Course, Note to Ex. 4 in Exercise 1 of the Forty Exercises"). Some writers also omit ling. As a matter of principle, in cases of this kind uniformity should be observed; ling should either be always used to replace zero (except at the end of a number), or it should be always omitted. Ling is also used to indicate a gap in the series of decimal weights or money, etc., e.g. 六 两 零 八 分 liu liang ling pa fên, six taels and eight candareens. The ling here indicates that a decimal, viz. that of the mace, is not represented.

(127) In stating amounts of money if there are no fractional amounts, i.e. no mace, candareens or cash, after the taels, the character 正 chêng, "exactly," for which 整 chêng is used in the Ta-hsieh style, is sometimes added, in order to prevent the unauthorised addition of other characters, just as we add the word "only" to round numbers of coin on cheques and similar documents.

關¹ 平² 銀³ 四⁴ 百⁵ 兩⁶ 正⁷—¹kuan-²p'ing ³yin Haikuan silver ⁶liang Taels ⁴ssŭ-⁵pai four hundred ⁷chêng exactly, or "Haikuan Taels four hundred only." ⁷chêng would have to be omitted if there were some fraction of a tael coming after ⁶liang.

(128) If numbers are distinctly meant to be left uncertain, *i.e.* if we would say "about so many" or "so much more or less," the phrases 左右 *tso-yu*, *lit.* left or right, and 不等 *pu-têng* sometimes follow the numeral expression, *e.g.*

如¹ 果² 漢³ 口⁴ 行⁵ 情⁶ 在⁷ 四⁸ 兩⁹ 左¹⁰ 右¹¹ 祈¹² 代¹³ 辦¹⁴ 一¹⁵ 百¹⁶ 桶¹⁷—¹*ju-*²*kuo* if ⁵*hang-*⁶*ch'ing* hong-matters *i.e.* the market price ³*han-*⁴*k'ou* at Hankow ⁷*tsai* is at ⁸*ssŭ* four ⁹*liang* Taels ¹⁰*tso-*¹¹*yu* more or less, ¹²*shih* pray ¹⁴*pan* buy ¹³*tai* for (me) ¹⁵*i-*¹⁶*pai* a hundred ¹⁷*t'ung* casks. "If the Hankow market has come down to about four Taels I shall be obliged by your buying for me a hundred casks (of Wood Oil) [402].

一¹ 甲² 之³ 戶⁴ 往⁵ 往⁶ 相⁷ 隔⁸ 數⁹ 十¹⁰ 里¹¹ 不¹² 等¹³— ⁴*hu* the families ³*chih* of ¹*i* one ²*chia* tithing ⁵*wang-*⁶*wang* constantly ⁷*hsiang-*⁸*chieh* are separated from each other ¹²*pu-* ¹³*têng* about, more or less ⁹*shu-*¹⁰*shih* several times ten ¹¹*li* Li, Chinese miles. "—The families forming a tithing are constantly scores of *li* or so apart from each other" (107).

(129) This phrase 不等 *pu-têng* has disjunctive force when following *two* numbers, as 二三兩不等 *êrh san liang pu-têng*, two OR three Taels.*

各¹ 給² 錢³ 二⁴ 三⁵ 百⁶ 至⁷ 八⁸ 九⁹ 百¹⁰ 文¹¹ 不¹² 等¹³— ¹*ko* each ²*chi* gave, paid ³*ch'ien* of money ⁴*êrh* ⁵*san* two OR three ⁶*pai* hundred ⁷*chih* up to ⁸*pa* ⁹*chiu* eight OR nine ¹*pai* hundred ¹¹*wên* cash ¹²*pu-*¹³*têng* (expressing OR ou the two previous occasions). "Every man paid so much; some of them 200 or 300, some 800 or 900, cash apiece" [209].†

* It is, in this sense, not confined to numbers, but may follow other words as well, *e.g.* 大小不等 *ta-hsiao pu-têng*, largo OR small.

† According to Rémusat we should place under this category the character 餘 *yü* which very frequently follows a numeral expression. "Quand on exprime un nombre dont on n'entend pas garantir la précision, on y ajoute 餘 *iú* on 許 *hiù*, qui signifient *environ*, *un peu plus ou un peu moins*". *Grammaire Chinoise*, p. 51. The following example, however, shows clearly the meaning of this word to be "MORE THAN," the

(130) Ordinals are expressed by placing the character 第 i.e. number, before the ordinary numeral, as 第五 *ti-wu*, No. 5, i.e. the fifth. The ordinal numbers used to mark the first ten days of the month are composed with 初 *ch'u*, as 初一日 *ch'u-i jih*, the first of the month; 初十日 *ch'u-shih jih*, the tenth.

(131) 初 *ch'u* has by itself the meaning of an ordinal number in the sense of "first," e.g. 初旬 *ch'u hsün*, the first decade, the first ten days of a month; 初次 *ch'u-tz,ŭ* the first time.

(132) 第一 *ti-i*, the first, placed before a noun has superlative power, as in 第一等 No. 1 class, the first class = the best.

以¹ 保² 固³ 民⁴ 心⁵ 爲⁶ 第⁷ 一⁸ 義⁹—¹*i...⁶wei* to consider ²*pao-*³*ku* ⁴*min-*⁵*hsin* protecting the heart of the people is ⁷*ti-*⁹*i* ⁹*i* the foremost, the best principle. —"The security of the popular mind against alarm is the foremost of essentials" (102; cf. 426 col. 5).

(133) Ordinals are, however, quite frequently expressed by simple cardinals whenever no misunderstanding can arise from the omission of 第 *ti*. This is, for instance, regularly the case with all dates, e.g.

光¹ 緒² 六³ 年⁴ 十⁵ 月⁶ 二⁷ 十⁸ 三⁹ 日¹⁰—⁷*ėrh-*⁸*shih-*⁹*san*

opposite of 不足 *pu-tsu* placed before the number, i.e. "LESS THAN," and not "about" or "more or less."

十¹ 家² 一³ 牌⁴ 此⁵ 定⁶ 式⁷ 也⁸ 亦⁹ 有¹⁰ 不¹¹ 足¹² 十¹³ 家¹⁴ 者¹⁵ 亦¹⁶ 有¹⁷ 十¹⁸ 餘¹⁹ 家²⁰ 者²¹ 任²² 其²³ 量²⁴ 地²⁵ 一
¹*shih* ten ²*chia* families ³*i* one ⁴*p'ai* ticket; ⁵*tz'ŭ* this ⁸*yeh* is ⁶*ting*.⁷*shih* the standing rule; ¹⁰*yu* there are ⁹*yeh* also ¹⁵*chė* such which are, contain ¹¹*pu-*¹²*tsu* not enough to, i.e. less than ¹³*shih* ten ¹⁴*chia* families; ¹⁷*yu* there are ¹⁶*yeh* also ²¹*chė* such which contain ¹⁹*yü* MORE THAN ¹⁸*shih* ten ²⁰*chia* families; (we should) ²²*jėn* allow ²³*ch'i* these ²⁴*liang* to measure ²⁵*ti* the ground. "The standing rule is that there shall be a [large] ticket to every ten families; but there are cases in which there may be more than ten families or less, and in such cases allowance must be made, and [the tithing declared] by measurement of ground" [112].

餘 *yü* has here decidedly the meaning of 多 *to* in the example 一百多人 *i-pai to jėn*, MORE than 100 men.

THE twenty-third [10]*jih* day of [5]*shih* THE tenth [6]*yüeh* moon of [8]*liu* THE sixth [4]*nien* year of [1]*kuang*-[2]*hsü* the Emperor Kuang-hsü.

該[1] 船[2] 二[3] 伙[4],—[3]*ĕrh* the second [4]*huo* mate of [1]*kai* the said, that [2]*ch'uan* vessel.*

(134) "The second" may be expressed by 次 *tz'ŭ* in certain combinations, as in 次日 *tz'ŭ-jih*, the second or following day (72 col. 5); 次早 *tz'ŭ tsao*, the next morning; 次玉 *tz'ŭ yü*, a second class, i.e. an inferior gem; 次硝 *tz'ŭ hsiao*, second class, i.e. inferior saltpetre.

(135) Otherwise this character 次 *tz'ŭ* is used in forming multiplicative numbers; it corresponds to the English "*times*" in " five times" (五 次 *wu tz'ŭ*).

兩 次 *liang tz'ŭ*=twice: 經[1] 該[2] 府[3] 兩[4] 次[5] 委[6] 員[7] 審[8] 辦[9]—[2]*kai* the said, the [3]*fu* Prefect [1]*ching* (sign of the past) has [4]*liang*-[5]*tz'ŭ* twice [6]*wei* deputed [7]*yüan* an officer to [8]*shĕn*-[9]*pan* try the case (32).

二 次 *ĕrh-tz'ŭ*=twice: 輸稅二次 *shu shui ĕrh-tz'ŭ*, to pay duty twice (17).

一 次 *i-tz'ŭ*, once; 每一次 *mei i-tz'ŭ* each time; 三 次 *san-tz'ŭ*, three times, etc.

此 次 *tz'ŭ-tz'ŭ* means "this time" (339); 疊 次 *tieh-tz'ŭ*, repeatedly (3 col. 9); 屢 次 *lü-tz'ŭ*, 節 次 *chieh-tz'ŭ*, 累 次 *lei-tz'ŭ*, 連 次 *lien-tz'ŭ*, 多 次 *to-tz'ŭ*, 歷 次 *li-tz'ŭ*, many times, often; 前 次 *ch'ien-tz'ŭ* occurs with the meaning "a previous time," "on a former occasion,"—" already" (*cf.* Wade's Note 4 to Paper 41). Functions similar to those of 次 *tz'ŭ* are performed by the characters 回 *hui*, 番 *fan*, and 遭 *ts'ao*.

* I have seen a translation in which the rendering of the above example by "the two mates of that ship" was about to create a serious confusion in a criminal case. To express this last meaning the Chinese writer would have said:

該[1] 船[2] 大[3] 二[4] 伙[5] 兩[6] 人[7]—[3]*ta* the first and [4]*ĕrh* the second [5]*huo* mate of [1]*kai* that [2]*ch'uan* vessel, [6]*liang* both [7]*jĕn* men.

(136)   Another multiplicative character is 倍 *pei*.

擬¹ 罰² 正³ 稅⁴ 三⁵ 倍⁶—¹*i-*²*fa* he was fined ⁵*san-*⁶*pei* three times ³*chêng-*⁴*shui* the full duty.

Note that the multiplicand (³*chêng-*⁴*shui*) is placed before the multiplicator (⁵*san*).

(137)   Distributive numbers are simply formed by the addition of 每 *mei*, each, every.

每¹ 十² 戶³ 合⁴ 訂⁵ 一⁶ 冊⁷—¹*mei* every ²*shih* ten ³*hu* families ⁴*ho-*⁵*ting* unite to constitute ⁶*i* one ⁷*ts'ê* register. "Every ten families must make up a register" (111).

This form is also used to express *percentage*.

瓦¹ 器² 僅³ 照⁴ 估⁵ 價⁶ 每⁷ 百⁸ 兩⁹ 抽¹⁰ 稅¹¹ 五¹² 兩¹³—¹*wa-*²*ch'i* earthen ware ¹⁰*ch'ou* ¹¹*shui* is levied duty ³*chin* only ¹²*wu* ¹³*liang* five taels ⁴*chao* according to ⁵*ku-*⁶*chia* value ⁷*mei* of every, PER ⁸*pai* hundred ⁹*liang* Taels ; "earthenware only pays an *ad valorem* duty of five per cent" (12).

(138)   *Fractions* may be expressed with 分 *fên*, part, *e.g.* 三¹ 分² 之³ 二⁴, ⁴*êrh* two ³*chih* of ¹*san* three ²*fên* parts, *i.e.* two thirds.

舊¹ 商² 買³ 賣⁴ 不⁵ 及⁶ 新⁷ 商⁸ 百⁹ 分¹⁰ 之¹¹ 一¹²,—³*mai-*⁴*mai* the trade of ¹*chiu* the old ²*shang* merchants ⁵*pu-*⁶*chi* does not reach up to ¹²*i* one ¹¹*chih* of ⁹*pai* hundred ¹⁰*fên* parts of [that of] ⁷*hsin-*³*shang* the new merchants. "Trade in former times was not the hundredth part so extensive as it is now" (385).

(139)   The omission of 分 *fên* is, however, quite usual so that nothing but the Genitive relation remains to indicate the fraction.

天¹ 下² 銅³ 斤⁴ 產⁵ 於⁶ 滇⁷ 者⁸ 十⁹ 之¹⁰ 五¹¹ 六¹² 產¹³ 他¹⁴ 省¹⁵ 者¹⁶ 十¹⁷ 之¹⁸ 三¹⁹ 四²⁰—¹*t'ien-*²*hsia* ³*t'ung-*⁴*chin* of the world's copper, of all the copper produced in the Empire ⁸*chê* that which ⁵*ch'an* is produced ⁶*yü* in ⁷*tien* Yünnan [is, makes, constitutes] ¹¹*wu* ¹²*liu* five or six [parts] ¹⁰*chih* of, out of ^9shih ten; $^{16}ch\hat{e}$ that which $^{13}ch'an$ is produced in $^{14}t'a$ other $^{15}sh\hat{e}ng$ provinces ^{19}san $^{20}ss\check{u}$ three or four [parts] $^{18}chih$ out of $^{17}shih$ ten. "Yünnan furnishes five or six tenths, other provinces three or four tenths of all the copper produced in China" (347).

NUMERALS EMPLOYED IN FORMING IDIOMATIC PHRASES.

— i, ONE

(140) In addition to the various uses of this character already described the following should be noted:

1. — i often corresponds to our indefinite article, a; an
2. — — i-i=one by one (= 逐 — chu-i).

且^1 有^2 戶^3 書^4 某^5 姓^6 於^7 民^8 等^9 建^{10} 造^{11} 事^{12} 情^{13} —^{14} —^{15} 洞^{16} 悉^{17}—$^1ch'ieh$ further ^2yu there is ^3hu-^4shu the revenue clerk ^5mao ^6hsing so and so $^{16}tung$-^{17}hsi is thoroughly acquainted ^{14}i-^{15}i one by one, point for point, in detail $^7y\ddot{u}$ with $^{10}chien$ $^{11}tsao$ $^{12}shih$-$^{13}ch'ing$ the matter of house building of ^8min-$^9t\check{e}ng$ petitioners. "[If farther testimony to the truth of their statement be needed,] there is C.D., clerk in the Revenue Office who knows the whole story of petitioner's house building" (58).

必^1 須^2 逐^3 —^{4} 查^5 實^6—Circumstances ^1pi-$^2hs\ddot{u}$ must be $^5ch'a$-^6shih ascertained ^3chu-^4i, one by one, in detail. "The real reason why, etc., should EACH AND ALL be ascertained" (100).

3. —..., —..., —..., i..., i..., i...=the one..., the other ..., the third..., etc. [33 cols 5 and 6].

4. — 則..., — 則..., i-$ts\hat{o}$..., i-$ts\hat{o}$=firstly..., secondly ..., etc.

5. 無^1 —^{2} 不^3,—^1wu there is not ^2i one ^3pu who does not ...i.e. everyone does, e.g.

無^1 —^{2} 丁^3 —^{4} 家^5 不^6 受^7 轄^8 於^9 社^{10} 廟^{11} 者^{12}—^1wu there is not ^2i one ^3ting individual [nor] ^4i one ^5chia family ^6pu $^{12}ch\hat{e}$ who does not ^7shou receive ^8hsia orders, i.e. who is not under the authority, $^9yü$ of $^{10}shê$-$^{11}miao$ the local deity temple. "—there is not a family nor an individual over whom the temple has not authority" (107).

6. 不一 pu-i, 非一 fei-i, not of one kind, i.e. many-fold: 其¹ 害² 不³ 一⁴—²hai the injuries ¹$ch'i$ of it, done by it ³pu-⁴i are not of one kind, i.e. are many-fold.

舞¹ 弊² 之³ 人⁴ 非⁵ 一⁶ 類⁷—Of ⁴$jên$ men ³$chih$ who ¹wu-²pi wink at malpractices ⁵fei there is not ⁶i one ⁷lei class. "There are many who wink at malpractices" (264).

7. 一 帶 i-tai, lit. the whole belt or line; the neighbourhood.

余¹ 山² 東³ 北⁴ 一⁵ 帶⁶ 係⁷ 兵⁸ 船⁹ 未¹⁰ 便¹¹ 駛¹² 往¹³ 之¹⁴ 處¹⁵—⁵i-⁶$t'ai$ the neighbourhood, the whole region ³$tung$-⁴pei north-east of ¹$shê$-²$shan$ Shê-shan ⁷hsi is ¹⁵$ch'u$ a place ¹⁴$chih$ of, here: to which ⁸$ping$-⁹$ch'uan$ men-of-war ¹⁰wei-¹¹$pien$ ought not to ¹²$shih$-¹³$wang$ proceed. "The ground north-west of the Shê Shan is ground to which men-of-war should properly not go" (21).

勾¹ 結² 五³ 排⁴ 一⁵ 帶⁶ 匪⁷ 類⁸—They ¹kou-²$chieh$ connect with ⁷fei-⁸lei the outlaws of ⁵i-⁶$t'ai$ the neighbourhood of ³wu-⁴$p'ai$ Wu P'ai. They "join the outlaws of the Wu P'ai country" (103; cf. 254 col. 1).

8. 萬一 wan-i, ten thousand to one, i.e. most probably, almost certainly (357 col. 2).

9. If documents are divided into sections or articles, each article may be headed by — i, which should, of course, be left untranslated. As in treaties and similar documents there are many occasions to break the text by commencing a new column by the rules of diplomatic etiquette,* the mere beginning of a fresh column, otherwise corresponding to our commencing a new paragraph, would not be a sufficient guide

---

* See Mayers' notes on the Chinese system of Distinctive collocation of Characters on p. 121 of "The Chinese Government," Shanghai, 1876.

in distinguishing between the different articles. The character — *i*, has, therefore, been introduced here as a mark only, and is often raised by the space of one character as for instance in the Chinese text of the British Treaty of Tientsin. If, as in the French Treaty, nearly every article begins with the same word (凡, *fan*: *whenever* a French subject, etc.), this is in itself a sufficient mark of distinction; and the numbering of paragraphs renders the use of any other mark superfluous as *e.g.* in the Russian Treaty. The use of — *i*, however, is not only a thoroughly Chinese arrangement, but also adds considerably to the good looks of a lengthy text whether written or printed. (*See* Wade's text pp. 396 to 400).

二 *érh*; 三 *san*.

(141) 不 二 *pu-érh* not two, *i.e.* unalterable, as in the phrase often found among the inscriptions on signboards: 不 二 價 *pu-érh-chia*, "not two prices," *i.e.* sales at fixed prices, or "no over-prizing."

再三 *tsai-san*, *lit.* again, *i.e.* twice, and three times; again and again, frequently.

三 思 *san-ssŭ*, *lit.* to think three times* to think a matter over, to consider before acting (439 col. 7).

(142) The so-called *Numeral Phrases* constitute a special chapter among the forms of Chinese thought. As, beyond their frequent occurrence in the text, they do not affect the style of the language from a grammatical point of view, reference is here made to the complete collection forming Part II of Mayers' "The Chinese Reader's Manual."

(143) Certain characters are used *in lieu* of numerals and may be compared to our series of letters, A, B, C, etc. The volumes of a book, or in fact any other division of a literary

---

* It should be noted that, before verbs, simple numerals are sufficient to express multiplicative numbers *See* Marshman, p. 464: *Adverbs of Number*.

work may be numbered by characters not being numerals otherwise. If there are but two divisions the first may be called 上 *shang*, the superior part, the second, 下 *hsia* the inferior part; three divisions are called 上 *shang*, superior (1st), 中 *chung*, middle (2nd), and 下 *hsia* (3rd). A combination of two of any of these three characters allows of a ninefold set of dissyllables which is occasionally used to represent the numerals 1 to 9, *viz.*

上 上 *shang-shang*, the first,
中 上 *chung-shang*, the second,
下 上 *hsia-shang*, the third,
上 中 *shang-chung*, the fourth,
中 中 *chung-chung*, the fifth,
下 中 *hsia-chung*, the sixth,
上 下 *shang-hsia*, the seventh,
中 下 *chung-hsia*, the eighth,
下 下 *hsia-hsia*, the nineth; also "the very last," "the very lowest" of any series.

(144) A sequence of four parts may be numbered by the first four characters in the Book of Changes, *viz.*

元 *yüan* (=1st), 亨 *hêng* (=2nd), 利 *li* (=3rd), and 貞 *chêng* (=4th).

(145) The so-called Ten Stems (十 干 *shih kan*, see Williams' *Syll. Dict.* p. 309) and the Twelve Branches (十二支 *shih-êrh chih*, ibid. p. 54), forming the Duodenary cycle of symbols (ibid. p. 355) are also used as quasi-numerals whether alone, *i.e.* the Ten Stems in series of ten parts, the Twelve Branches in series of twelve parts, or combined with each other and forming the Sexagenary cycle, in series of sixty parts, or less. Longer series may be numbered with the characters of the "Thousand Character Classic," (*Ch'ien-tzŭ-wên* 千字文) denoting the numbers 1 to 1,000, or with those of the "Hundred Surnames" (*Po-chia-hsing* 百家姓).

DOCUMENTARY STYLE.

The following is a list of the first hundred characters in either series.

	Ch'ien-tzŭ-wên.	Po-chia-hsing.		Ch'ien-tzŭ-wên.	Po-chia-hsing.		Ch'ien-tzŭ-wên.	Po-chia-hsing.		Ch'ien-tzŭ-wên.	Po-chia-hsing.
1	天	趙	26	餘	曹	51	巨	昌	76	帝	畢
2	地	錢	27	成	嚴	52	闕	馬	77	鳥	郝
3	元	孫	28	歲	華	53	珠	苗	78	官	鄔
4	黃	李	29	律	金	54	稱	鳳	79	人	安
5	宇	周	30	呂	魏	55	夜	花	80	皇	常
6	宙	吳	31	調	陶	56	光	方	81	始	樂
7	洪	鄭	32	陽	姜	57	果	俞	82	制	于
8	荒	王	33	雲	戚	58	珍	任	83	文	時
9	日	馮	34	騰	謝	59	李	袁	84	字	傅
10	月	陳	35	致	鄒	60	奈	柳	85	乃	皮
11	盈	褚	36	雨	喻	61	菜	酆	86	服	卞
12	昃	衛	37	露	柏	62	重	鮑	87	衣	齊
13	辰	蔣	38	結	水	63	芥	史	88	裳	康
14	宿	沈	39	為	竇	64	薑	唐	89	推	伍
15	列	韓	40	霜	章	65	海	費	90	位	余
16	張	楊	41	金	雲	66	鹹	廉	91	讓	元
17	寒	朱	42	生	蘇	67	河	岑	92	國	卜
18	來	秦	43	麗	潘	68	淡	薛	93	有	顧
19	暑	尤	44	水	葛	69	鱗	雷	94	虞	孟
20	往	許	45	玉	奚	70	潛	賀	95	陶	平
21	秋	何	46	出	范	71	羽	倪	96	唐	黃
22	收	呂	47	崑	彭	72	翔	湯	97	弔	和
23	冬	施	48	岡	郎	73	龍	滕	98	民	穆
24	藏	張	49	劍	魯	74	師	殷	99	伐	蕭
25	閏	孔	50	號	韋	75	火	羅	100	罪	尹

THE ADJECTIVES.

(146) Such words as are generally used to form an attributive addition before a noun may be called adjectives. To this class Marshman (on p. 269) and others even refer words,

otherwise nouns, used attributively like adjectives. Marshman speaks of three kinds of adjectives: *original adjectives*, or those originally intended to describe a quality as existing in some subject; those which being originally *substantives*, are used occasionally to describe certain qualities inherent in substantives; and those which may be termed *compound adjectives*.

Under the last named kind Marshman describes what has been treated upon in these Notes under the head of Genitive, and even the second class (Substantives used attributively) may be looked at as being in the genitive relation to the noun they precede. We shall here, therefore, deal with adjectives proper in the first instance.

(147) These may in English be used either attributively, as in "the good man," or predicatively, as in "the man is good." Both cases, of course, exist in Chinese. The difference is expressed by position: attributes are placed before the noun, predicates follow.* 善¹ 馬² ¹shan-²ma, a good horse, a gentle horse; 人¹ 善² ¹jên ²shan, the man is good. Position alone being sufficient in the second example, to show that ²shan is the predicate of the subject ¹jên, the verb substantive, is, becomes superfluous and is, therefore, omitted.

(148) Attributes are generally simply placed before their nouns if they consist of a single character; if such adjectives are made to consist of more characters, however, or if several adjectives belong to the same noun as attributes, they are frequently connected by 之 *chih*, the particle not only of the genitive, but of anteposition as denoting dependence on something following, as in 奸¹ 狡² 之³ 徒⁴ ¹chien

---

* Note the exceptional form mentioned by Schott on p. 57:—"Adjectives denoting *personal qualities* may *follow* their substantive, but never without being preceded by 爲 *wei* (to agree, esse) : 廣爲人廉 *kuang wei jên-lien*, Kuang erat homo liberalis."

villainous and ²*chiao* crafty ³*chih* (connecting the two adjectives with the following noun) ⁴*t'u* fellows, ruffians (262).

永¹ 遠² 之³ 利⁴ ¹*yung*-²*yüan* eternal ³*chih* (connecting the preceding compound adjective with) ⁴*li* profit (361).

(149)   A noun placed as a Genitive before another noun may, of course, receive the force of an adjective. In the business style, for instance, the word 洋 *yang*, properly "the open sea," occurs quite as commonly as an adjective in the sense of "foreign" as in its original meaning. We say 洋關 *yang kuan*, the foreign Customs, 洋貨 *yang huo*, foreign goods, etc. In this case it would be difficult to render *yang* by the genitive of a noun; in other cases we are at liberty to chose between this and the adjective mode of translation. 地方官 *ti-fang kuan*, for instance, may be translated by either "the authorities of the place," or "the local authorities."

(150)   An adjective may receive the force of an abstract noun if it is preceded by a Genitive (generally with 之 *chih*,) or another adjective.

天¹ 地² 之³ 大⁴—⁴*ta* the greatness, vastness ³*chih* of ¹*t'ien* heaven and ²*ti* earth.

實¹ 心² 願³ 通⁴ 舊⁵ 好⁶—³*yüan* to wish ¹*shih*-²*hsin* with a true heart, *i.e.* to sincerely desire, to ⁴*t'ung* connect ⁵*chiu* the old ⁶*hao* good, here: good feelings, friendliness.

" —[if His Excellency] be sincere in his desire to renew friendly relations..." (3).

(151)   Two adjectives of opposite meaning unite to form an abstract noun implying the relative state in the category indicated by the two adjectives, *e.g.*,

輕重 *ch'ing-chung*, light-heavy, *i.e.* weight.

長短 *ch'ang-tuan*, long-short, *i.e.* length.

高低 *kao-ti*, high-low, *i.e.* height.

多少 *to-shao*, in the business style more commonly 多寡 *to-kua*, many-few, *i.e.* quantity.

All such expression may be used in the interrogative sense. The last named expression, for instance, is not only used to denote the substantive "quantity," but may come to literally mean "how many?" or "how much?"

其¹ 易² 錢³ 多⁴ 寡⁵ 之⁶ 數⁷—¹*ch'i* the ⁷*shu* number ⁶*chih* of ⁴*to*-⁵*kua* the quantity of ³*ch'ien* the cash ²*i* exchanged. "The amount of cash exchanged" (245).

無¹ 論² 贓³ 數⁴ 多⁵ 寡⁶—¹*wu*-²*lun* no matter ⁶*to*-⁵*kua* how much, how large ⁴*shu* the number of ³*tsang* the pillage (is). "No matter how large the amount of pillage may be," "irrespective of amount," "no matter, how much there was of it," etc. (292, *cf.* 373 col. 9).

(152) It is a matter of course that words otherwise adjectives are to be looked upon as adverbs when they belong to a verb instead of a noun.*

大¹ 為² 州³ 縣⁴ 之⁵ 累⁶—²*wei* it is ¹*ta* very much ⁶*lei* an embarassment ⁵*chih* of ³*chou*-⁴*hsien* the districts. "It greatly embarasses the districts" (355).

茲¹ 巳² 大³ 愈⁴ ¹*tzŭ* now *i* (sign of the past) he has ³*ta* greatly ⁴*yü* improved; "he is now much better" (43). We say similarly:

今¹ 病² 小³ 愈⁴ *chin* now ²*ping* the disease (has) ³*hsiao* slightly ⁴*yü* improved; "his disease is now a little better" (Williams.)

In some cases, as will be seen from the above examples, this change of category involves a modification of the meaning; 大 *ta*, large, for instance has the force of an adverb of intensity when so employed.

---

* When adjectives are used as verbs they are usually pronounced in a different tone, as 好 *hao* *(shang-shêng)* good; *hao* *(ch'ü-shêng)*, to love; or a slight change takes place in the sound, as 惡 *ngo*, bad, which means "to hate" when pronounced *wu* (*ch'ü-shêng*).

尚¹未² 大³ 痊⁴—he has ¹shang-²wei not yet ³ta very much,
i.e. QUITE ⁴chüan recovered (43).

(153) The adjective 多 to, multus, multa, multum, etc.,
appears in some cases to be considered an adverb by the
Chinese, to judge from its position. For although it is found
to stand before nouns, too, it is generally given the position
of an adverb.

多 雇 工 匠 to ku kung-chiang instead of ku to kung ku"= to hire
chiang, to hire many workmen (276).   to others
                                              for

多¹ 帶² 兵³ 役⁴ 添⁵ 雇ᴶ 人⁷ 夫⁸—to ²tai take with one's self
¹to many ³ping-⁴i soldiers and ⁶ku hire ⁵tien additional ⁷jên-
⁸fu workmen (278). The Chinese says: to much-take with
one's self soldiers and to additionally-hire workmen, ⁵tien
being here similarly used as ¹to.*

多¹ 設² 水³ 缸⁴ 木⁵ 桶⁶—to ²shê establish, keep in readi-
ness ¹to many ³shui-⁴kang water-kongs and ⁵mu-⁶t'ung
wood casks (442).

(154) In these cases 多 to, in our translation, belongs to
the object following the verb. It may, however, claim its
right as an adverb by position, and then it should be rendered by " frequently," " in many instances," or some similar
phrase.

THE COMPARATIVE.

(155) Gützlaff has probably hit the truth in saying that
" we know of no language that adopts so many modes of
expressing the degrees of comparison as the Chinese." The
business style more especially takes advantage of this
abundance of the language to the fullest extent. The
following forms are in common use.

* 增 tsêng, additional, follows the same rule.
每¹ 段² 增³ 雇⁴ 人⁵ 夫⁶ 數¹ 百⁸ 名⁹—¹mei each ²tuan section (is
to) ⁴ku hire ³tsêng additional ⁵jên.⁶fu workmen, ⁷shu ⁸pai several hundred ⁹ming names, i.e. " each section is to hire several hundred additional men" (283).

更 kêng = MORE, *magis;* 比 *pi* and 較 *chiao* = THAN, *quam.*

(156) The simple comparative of an adjective may be formed by prefixing 更 *kêng*, more: 好 *hao*, good, 更好 *kêng-hao*, better. When two things are compared to each other with regard to the degree in which either of them possesses a certain quality, the object to which the other is compared, preceded by 比 *pi* or 較 *chiao*, follows the object compared, and the adjective describing the quality stands at the end, with or without 更 *kêng*, the former characters corresponding to *quam* in Latin, the English *than*.

番[1] 人[2] 造[3] 船[4] 比[5] 中[6] 國[7] 更[8] 固[9]—[4]*ch'uan* the vessels [3]*tsao* made, constructed by [1]*fan-*[2]*jên* foreigners (are) [8]*kêng-*[9]*ku* steadier [5]*pi* than [6]*chung-*[7]*kuo* China, *i.e.* Chinese vessels. "Foreigners build more solid ships than we Chinese" (319).

番[1] 山[2] 材[3] 木[4] 比[5] 內[6] 地[7] 更[8] 堅[9]—[3]*tsai-*[4]*mu* the timber of [1]*fan-*[2]*shan* foreign hills (is) [8]*kêng-*[9]*chien* more substantial [5]*pi* than [6]*nei-*[7]*ti* the interior, *i.e.* the timber brought from the interior of China (319).

其[1] 浙[2] 江[3] 幫[4] 船[5] 亦[6] 較[7] 蘇[8] 松[9] 稍[10] 遠[11]—[1]*ch'i* the *pang-*[5]*ch'uan* squadron of [2]*chê-*[3]*chiang* Chehkiang (is) [6]*yeh* also [10]*shao* rather [11]*yüan* distant [7]*chiao* when compared to [8]*su-*[9]*sung* Su-sung, *i.e.* that of the Suchou and Sungkiang Intendancy (277).

The last mentioned example shows that our translation of this form by the comparative is not always suitable inasmuch as, here, the original sense of the construction is somewhat concealed; we may bring it forward by saying: "the Chehkiang fleet is rather more distant than the Su-sung fleet, more so than suits our purpose," or "it is a little *too* far away from the Su-sung fleet."

現[1] 聞[2] 米[3] 價[4] 二[5] 兩[6] 有[7] 餘[8] 較[9] 下[10] 江[11] 尚[12] 貴[13]— [1]*hsien* now [2]*wên* we hear that [3]*mi-*[4]*chia* the price of rice, *viz.,* [5]*êrh* two [6]*liang* taels [7]*yu-*[8]*yü* and more (is) [12]*shang* still [13]*kuei* dearer ⁹*chiao* than ¹⁰*hsia-*¹¹*chiang* down the river, *i.e.* than it is in the lower Yangtze district (355).

尤 *yu*, STILL MORE.

(157) This character is similarly employed as 更 *kêng*, as the following example will show.

揆¹ 其² 情³ 節⁴ 似⁵ 較⁶ 白⁷ 鵬⁸ 鶴⁹ 之¹⁰ 案¹¹ 尤¹² 為¹³ 可¹⁴ 憫¹⁵—¹*K'uei* if we consider the ³*ch'ing-*⁴*chieh* circumstances ²*ch'i* of it, of this case, ⁵*ssŭ* it appears that ¹³*wei* it is ¹²*yu* still more ¹⁴*k'o-*¹⁵*mên* to be pitied, pitiable ⁶*chiao* than ¹¹*an* the case ¹⁰*chih* of ⁷*pai* ⁸*p'êng-*⁹*ho* Pai P'êng-ho.

"All these incidents being duly weighed, his case appears even more deserving of commiseration than that of Pai P'êng-ho" (203; *cf.* 325 col. 6).

尤甚 *yu-shên*, much more intense (280).

於 *yü*, THAN.

(158) This word, originally used as a preposition, has in certain combinations the sense of the Latin *quam*, and is sufficient to produce comparative force when following an adjective.

貴¹ 於² 銀³ ¹*kuei* dearer ²*yü* than ³*yin* silver.

礮¹ 火² 軍³ 械⁴ 精⁵ 於⁶ 中⁷ 土⁸—(Speaking of western nations:) in ¹*p'ao-*¹*huo* gunnery and ³*chün-*⁴*hsieh* military equipment (they are) ⁵*ching* more skilful ⁶*yü* than ⁷*chung-*⁸*t'u* China, *i.e.* the Chinese (316).

In negative sentences, or in interrogative sentences with negative force, this construction may come to replace the superlative, as if we were to say: "of men there was none greater than Yü," or "of men, who was greater than Yü?"—both forms meaning: "Yü was the greatest of men."

為¹ 治² 奠³ 要⁴ 於⁵ 安⁶ 民⁷ 安⁸ 民⁹ 奠¹⁰ 急¹¹ 於¹² 弭¹³ 盜¹⁴ —¹*wei-*²*chih* in governing ³*mo* there is not (anything) ⁴*yao* more important ⁵*yü* than ⁶*an-*⁷*min* to keep the people in peace; ⁸*an-*⁹*min* in keeping the people in peace ¹⁰*mo* there is nothing ^{11}ch'i more necessary ^{12}yü than ^{13}mi to keep down ^{14}tao the seditious.

"To keep the people in peace is the most important measure in the practice of government; the most urgent measure to obtain this end, is the keeping down of the seditious." (Yung-chêng's Edicts, 9th year, 7th moon).

滇^1 中^2 之^3 弊^4 莫^5 甚^6 於^7 鹽^8 而^9 滇^{10} 中^{11} 之^{12} 利^{13} 莫^{14} 大^{15} 於^{16} 銅^{17}—^{4}pi of the deficiencies ^{3}chih of ^{2}chung the within of ^{1}tien yünnau ^{5}mo there is none ^{6}shên more intense ^{7}yü than ^{8}yen salt ^{9}êrh and ^{13}li of the profits ^{12}chih of ^{11}chung the within of ^{10}tien Yünnan ^{14}mo there is none ^{15}ta greater ^{16}yü than ^{17}t'ung copper.

"As dearth of salt is the foremost grievance of the Yünnan people, abundance of copper is their greatest blessing" (347).

(159) 莫 mo, the negative particle commonly employed for this purpose may in such cases be replaced by 孰 shu= quis? Cf. Julien, p. 40.

愈 yü, MORE (quo magis : eo magis).

(160) Two adjectives (or verbs) either of which is preceded by the above character are to be considered as comparatives in correlation. 愈 yü then corresponds to the English word THE (originally an old Ablative or Instrumental case of the Demonstrative Pronoun THE, THAT, O. E. se, seo, thæt) in the example: "THE nearer the bone, THE sweeter the meat," or the Latin quo...eo..., or the German je... desto..., followed by comparatives.

愈^1 久^2 愈^3 紊^4—^{1}yü-^{2}chiu THE longer it lasts ^{3}yü-^{4}wên THE more confused (the matter gets) (353).

所^1 製^2 鐵^3 篩^4 筴^5 日^6 來^7 愈^8 用^9 愈^{10} 精^{11}—The ^{4}po-^{5}chi sieves ^{1}so which are ^{2}chih made of ^{3}tieh iron ^{6}jih-^{7}lai day by day, ^{8}yü-^{9}yung the more [they are] used ^{10}yü-^{11}ching the finer (they get).

DOCUMENTARY STYLE. 119

"Iron sieves become finer the longer they are used (359).
(161) This is the ordinary use of these characters; but 愈
simply placed before an adjective, may alone express the comparative, as 愈難 *yü-nan*, more difficult; 航船愈快 *hang ch'uan yü-kuai*, he sailed faster (Philosinensis), 愈甚 *yü-shên*=尤甚 *yu-shên*, much more, more intense.

寕 *ning*, RATHER : 不 *pu*, THAN.

(162) The first word is used to express a comparison between two actions of which the one introduced by it is represented as being preferable or better than the one compared, the latter being preceded by the negative particle 不 *pu*, e.g.

寕¹ 死² 不³ 去⁴ ¹*ning* rather ²*ssŭ* die ³*pu* and not ⁴*ch'ü* go, i.e. I would RATHER die THAN go.

寕¹ 死² 不³ 辱⁴ ¹*ning* I would rather, or "it is better to" ²*ssŭ* die ³*pu* than ⁴*ju* be dishonored." " I prefer death to disgrace."

寕¹ 可² 信³ 其⁴ 有⁵ 不⁶ 可⁷ 信⁸ 其⁹ 無¹⁰—*néng* potius ²*k'o* ³*hsin* credi potest, credendum ⁴*ch'i* illud ⁵*yu* esse ⁶*pu* quam ⁷*k'o-*³*hsin* credi possit, sit credendum ⁹*ch'i* illud ¹⁰*wu* non esse. " It is better to believe in its existence than to believe in its non-existence."

不 如 *pu ju* : 不 若 *pu jo* ; 莫 如 *mo ju* ; etc.,
"THERE IS NOTHING LIKE" "IS NOT LIKE, IS NOT SO GOOD AS"etc.
(163) The comparative particles 如 *ju* and 若 *jo*, when preceded by the negation, frequently denote a sort of preferableness in the subject considered. (Prémare, p. 209. Julien translates this phrase by : *il vaut mieux*. Syntaxe Nouvelle, pp. 238 and 290).

莫¹ 若² 修³ 其⁴ 本⁵—¹*mo-*²*jo* there is nothing like ³*hsiu* cultivating ⁴*ch'i* of it ⁵*pên* the root, " there is nothing like cultivating the root." (Prémare).

指¹ 不² 若³ 人⁴—¹*chih* the finger ²*pu-*³*jo* is not so good as ⁴*jên* the man. "Le doigt ne vaut pas l'homme entier" (Julien).

不¹ 如² 乘³ 勢⁴—¹pu-²ju il vaut miex ³shˑng profiter de ⁴shih l'occasion (Julien).

盜¹ 匪² 雖³ 多⁴ 不⁵ 如⁶ 士⁷ 民⁸ 善⁹ 良¹⁰ 之¹¹ 衆¹²—¹tao-²fei the robbers, ³sui though ⁴to many, ⁵pu-⁶ju are not like ¹²chung the multitude ¹¹chih of ⁹shan-¹⁰liang the good ones, loyal subjects of ⁷shih-⁸min the literati and common people, i.e. "the robbers, though numerous, are LESS in number, etc."

"Robbers may be numerous, but their number is not equal to that of the respectable classes, the literati and the people" (110).

伊¹ 己² 年³ 老⁴ 無⁵ 用⁶ 不⁷ 如⁸ 服⁹ 毒¹⁰—¹i she (being) ²i already ³nien-⁴lao old and ⁵wu-⁶yung of no use ⁷pu-⁸ju she had better, ⁹fu-¹⁰tu take poison.

An old woman says: "being old and useless, she had better poison herself" (225).

與¹ 其² 遲³ 到⁴ 不⁵ 如⁶ 不⁷ 到—⁵pu-⁶ju it is better ⁷pu-⁸tao not to come ¹yü THAN ²ch'i the ³hsi-⁴tao late-coming, i.e. than to come late; the reversion of the English proverb: better late than never. "It is better not to come at all than to come late" (Philosinensis).

與¹ 其² 懲³ 辦⁴ 於⁵ 事⁶ 後⁷ 莫⁸ 如⁹ 防¹⁰ 範¹¹ 於¹² 未¹³ 形¹⁴—⁸mo-⁹ju it is better to ¹⁰fang-¹¹fan take preventive measures ¹²yü at the time of (matters) ¹³wei not having ¹⁴hsing taken a positive shape yet ¹yü THAN ²ch'i (being a sort of article to the following verbal expression, corresponding to the Greek τὸ) to ³chêng-⁴pan inflict punishment ⁵yü... ⁷hou after ⁶shih matters, i.e. after excesses have been committed.

"We had better take preventive measures before matters have taken a positive shape than inflict punishment after excesses have been committed" (281).*

* NOTE the use of 與 yü and 其 ch'i in the above two examples. Cf. Pré.

The Superlative.

(164) The Chinese language is, comparatively speaking, rich in particles meaning *very, extremely*, etc., which being placed before an adjective give it a sort of superlative force. The following may be met with in documents: 最 *tsui*, 極 *chi*, 甚 *shên*, 至 *chih*, 殊 *shu*, 切 *ch'ich*, 絕 *chüeh*, 儘 *chin*, 深 *shên*, 大 *ta*, 綦 *ch'i*, 從 *ts'ung*. It may suffice to illustrate the use of a few of them by examples.

最 *tsui*, Very, most.

(165) 南¹ 洋² 番³ 族¹ 最⁵ 多⁶—the ³*fan*-⁴*lü* foreign tribes of ¹*nan*-²*yang* the Southern Ocean (are) ⁵*tsui*-⁶*to* very numerous (315).

東¹ 方² 之³ 國⁴ 日⁵ 本⁶ 最⁷ 爲⁸ 强⁹ 大¹⁰—Of ⁴*kuo* the countries ³*chih* of ¹*tung*-²*fang* the east ⁵*jih*-⁶*pên* Japan ⁸*wei* is ⁷*tsui* the most ⁹*chiang*-¹⁰*ta* powerful (315).

It will be observed that the position of *tsui* 最 is here affected by the verb *wei* 爲.* A different position again rules in the following example:

暹¹ 羅² 爲³ 西⁴ 南⁵ 之⁶ 最⁷—¹*hsien*-²*lo* Siam ³*wei* is ⁷*tsui* the most extreme ⁶*chih* of, in ⁴*hsi*-⁵*nan* the south west (315).

甚 *shên*, Very.

(166) This is the most common particle of intensifying force; it is quite as frequent in the business style as 狠 *hên*, very, is in the Mandarin colloquial.

甚 好 *shên-hao*, very good.

mare p. 198, § 6. 不 如 *pu-ju* and 莫 如 *mo-ju* here apparently correspond to 寧 *ning* in the example quoted by Prémare: 與 其 不 孫 也 寧 固 *yü ch'i pu sun yeh ning ku*, it is better to appear rude than to be, proud and haughty. Prémare adds: "Observe that the characters are always arranged in the same manner."

* Other adverbs such as 大 *ta*, 甚 *shên*, 深 *shên*, 尤 *yu* are given a similar position, *e.g.* 尤¹ 爲² 切³ 要⁴ ²*wei* it is ¹*yu* still more ³*ch'ieh*-⁴*yao* important. 其¹ 利² 最³ 爲⁴ 不⁵ 小⁶—¹*ch'i*.²*li* the advantage of this ⁴*wei* is ³*shên* in a high degree ⁵*pu*-⁶*hsiao* not small, *i.e.* very great.

其¹ 費² 甚³ 大⁴—¹ch'i its ²fei expenses (are) ³shên very ⁴ta large (348).

編¹ 甲² 甚³ 非⁴ 易⁵ 易⁶ 豈⁷ 數⁸ 旬⁹ 所¹⁰ 能¹¹ 畢¹² 事¹³—¹pien-²chia registration under the tithing system (is) ³shên-⁴fei very much not, i.e. by no means ⁵i-⁶i very easy; ⁷ch'i how is it, i.e. it is not ¹³shih a matter ¹⁰so which ¹¹nêng can ¹²pi be finished ⁸shu-⁹hsün within a few decades.

"Under these circumstances, registration under the tithing system is far from an easy matter; it is not a question that can be definitely disposed of in a few weeks" (107).

深 shên, DEEPLY, VERY.

(167) This word, similar in sound and meaning to, is almost as commonly used as, the former. From its original meaning "deep" it has become an intensifying particle like the English equivalent in phrases like "deeply regretted," though its use as an adverb is much wider in Chinese.

深¹ 爲² 隱³ 憂⁴—²wei he is ¹shên deeply, very much ³yin-⁴yu afflicted, "he is seriously distressed" (18).

深¹ 以² 所³ 稟⁴ 爲⁵ 然⁶—²i-⁵wei I consider ³so ⁴ping that which is stated as ¹shên ⁶jan very much so. "I consider there is much truth in what you state."

老¹ 弟² 愛³ 我⁴ 至⁵ 深⁶—¹lao-²ti the old brother, i.e. you ³ai like ⁴wo me ⁵chih-⁶shên very much (339).

Note the position of shên in the above examples.

至 chih, 極 chi, EXTREMELY, MOST.

(168) 至好 chih-hao, the best; 至聖 chih-shêng, most holy; 至誠 chih-ch'êng, most sincere; 至關緊要 chih kuan chin-yao highly important; 是¹ 爲² 至³ 要⁴ ¹shih this ²wei is ³chih most ⁴yao important; 至不仁 chih pu-jên most inhumane.

(169) 至極 chih-chi, the very extreme: 享福至極 hsiang-fu chih-chi he enjoyed great happiness (Philosinensis); 極多 chi-to, very many, too many; 極高明 chi-kao

ming most illustrious (Prémare); 極粗瓦器 *chi-tsu wa-ch'i*, the coarsest pottery (12).

極¹ 西² 則³ 紅⁴ 毛⁵—¹*chi-*²*hsi* in the extreme west ³*tsê* (particle of inference, here not translateable) (there are) ⁴*hung-*⁵*mao* the red-haired people, etc. (315).

殊 *shu*, 儘 *chin*, 絕 *chüeh*, EXTREMELY, MOST; VERY.

(170) 殊多 *shu-to*, very many; 殊異 *shu-i* very strange, most extraordinary; 殊未畫一 *shu wei hua i*, very dissimilar, the reverse of uniformity; 殊可恨 *shu k'o-hên*, most hateful (Philosinensis); 殊可憫 *shu k'o-min*, most lamentable (129); 殊¹ 屬² 疎³ 縱⁴ ²*shu* is ¹*shu* most ³*shu-*⁴*tsung* careless, very neglectful; 殊¹ 屬² 不³ 合⁴, (it) ²*shu* is ¹*shu* very ³*pu-*⁴*ho* unreasonable, unfair: "utterly inconsistent with right" (11; *cf.* 434 col. 1).

(171) 儘應 *chin-ying*, very proper: 儘東 *chin-tung*, easternmost; 儘先 *chin-hsien*, the first.

絕妙 *chüeh-miao*, most admirable; 絕美 *chüeh-mei*, extremely beautiful (Philosinensis).

綦 *ch'i*, 從 *ts'ung*, VERY.

(172) 綦嚴 *ch'i-yen*, very strict; 人¹ 命² 關³ 係⁴ 綦⁵ 重⁶ ³*kuan-*⁴*hsi* the consequences concerned in ¹*jên* man's ²*ming* life (are) ⁵*ch'i-*⁶*chung* very heavy; "the murder of man is a question of the gravest interest" (35).

從¹ 重² 究³ 辦⁴—³*chiu-*⁴*pan* to prosecute and punish ¹*ts'ung-*²*chung* most severely.

如 *ju*, 若 *jo*, 猶 *yu*, = LIKE *(adverbs of comparison)*.

(173) The first two of these particles frequently correspond to the English "like" as in the sentence: he fought LIKE a tiger; the last named (*yu*), Rémusat says on p. 95, marks the identity of two things, or of two words, being equivalents of each other. It appears that as adverbs of comparison they all have more or less the same meaning viz., like, according to, as.

愛¹ 民² 如³ 子⁴ 保⁵ 民⁶ 若⁷ 赤⁸—¹ai to love ²min the people ²ju like ⁴tzŭ children, one's own children; ⁵pao to protect ⁶min the people ⁷jo like ⁸ch'ih the naked (63).

如 何 ju-ho, like what, how, in what manner; the manner how—

可¹ 見² 該³ 國⁴ 究⁵ 係⁶ 外⁷ 夷⁸ 其⁹ 辦¹⁰ 事¹¹ 不¹² 能¹³ 如¹⁴ 中¹⁵ 國¹⁶ 之¹⁷ 有¹⁸ 條¹⁹ 有²⁰ 理²¹ 一²² 案²³ 必²⁴ 須²⁵ 一²⁶ 結²⁷ 也²⁸—¹k'o-²chien it may be seen, it is apparent (that) ³kai-⁴kuo that country (Annam) ⁶hsi is ⁵chiu after all ⁷wai-⁸i . . outer-barbarian (place); ¹¹shih the affairs ¹⁰pan managed ⁹ch'i by them ¹²pu-¹³nêng cannot ¹⁸yu-¹⁹t'iao-²⁰yu-²¹li have rule and law ¹⁴ju like ¹⁷ch'ih those of ¹⁵chung-¹⁶kuo China: ²²i-²³an a case ²⁴pi-²⁵hsü must (have) ²⁶i-²⁷chieh a conclusion ²⁸yeh (final particle).

"This shows that Annam is after all a barbarian country, that we cannot expect its affairs to be managed according to a fixed rule as in China where every case must be brought to an official conclusion" (377).

當¹ 面² 將³ 前⁴ 銀⁵ 如⁶ 數⁷ 交⁸ 清⁹—(a firm is to) ⁸chiao-⁹ch'ing pay ³chiang, (sign of the object) ⁴ch'ien-⁵yin the before-mentioned money ⁶ju-⁷shu AS PER number, i.e. in full ¹tang-²mien at once and in the presence of the recipient, i.e. on sight (of a certain bill of exchange) (95).

NEGATIVES.

(174) 不 pu, 無 wu, 非 fei, 未 wei; 莫 mo, 毋 wu, 勿 wu; 弗 fu, 否 fou; 罔 wang, 靡 mi.

The above is a longer list of negative particles than most other languages will be able to produce; it is not even quite complete, inasmuch as negatives peculiar to the colloquial and a few others not commonly used in the documentary style have been excluded from it. The first four are those chiefly used, and it is with them that we shall deal in the first instance.

DOCUMENTARY STYLE. 125

不 *pu*, Not.

(175) This is the simple negative and the one chiefly used before verbs, adverbs and adjectives. Its position is immediately before the word (verb or adjective) to which it applies.* It often enters into combination with adjectives of a positive sense to form what we would express by an adjective of negative meaning as if we were to say "not good" instead of "bad," and corresponds to the privative prefixes *un* (as in *un*wise), *in* (as in *in*tolerable), *dis* (as in *dis*similar), etc.

不¹ 敢² 回³ 籍⁴—they ²*kan* venture ¹*pu* not,—they do not dare to ³*hui*-⁴*chi* return to their home (129).

如¹ 此² 不³ 惟⁴ 與⁵ 原⁶ 議⁷ 不⁸ 符⁹ 而¹⁰ 且¹¹ 銀¹² 少¹³ 工¹⁴ 多¹⁵ 實¹⁶ 係¹⁷ 不¹⁸ 敷¹⁹ 竣²⁰ 工²¹ 之²² 用²³—¹*ju*-²*tz'ŭ* like this, thus ³*pu*-⁴*wei* not only [things will] ⁸*pu*-⁹*fu* not agree ⁵*yü* with ⁶*yüan*-⁷*i* the original plan, ¹⁰*êrh*-¹¹*ch'ieh* but also ¹²*yin*-¹³*shao*-¹⁴*kung*-¹⁵*to* money being little, work being much, ¹⁶*shih* ¹⁷*hsi* it will really ¹⁸*pu* not ¹⁹*fu* suffice for ²⁰*yung* the use, the purpose of ²⁰*chün*-²¹*kung* completing the work.

"Not only is this at variance with the understanding to which your petitioners were a party, but, as the work to be done will cost more than the sum allowed, that sum will not suffice for the completion of the work" (56).

不 足 *pu-tsu*, not enough, INsufficient, DEficient, *e.g.* 國家用 不 足 *kuo-chia pu-tsu*, a deficit in the budget.

不 安 *pu-an*, not at rest, UNeasy.

不 正 *pu-chêng*, not correct, INcorrect.

不 同 *pu-t'ung*, not the same, DIfferent.

不 妥 *pu-t'o*, not safe, UNsafe.

不 幸 *pu-hsing*, not fortunately, *i.e.* UNfortunately.

---

* The exceptional position by which a pronoun is placed between the negation and its verb (*e.g.* 不 吾 知 *pu wu chih*, "non mo novit," Schott p. 63, or "non ego noscor," Endlicher p. 247) is apparently confined to the *Ku-wên*, or used in imitation of the latter only.

不論 *pu-lun*
不拘 *pu-chü* } no matter.

不久 *pu-chiu*, not long, before long.

The phrases 不若 *pu-jo*, 不如 *pu-ju* have been mentioned in paragr. 163. As idiomatic, the following phrases may be noted.

不法 *pu-fa* (=無法 *wu-fa*) not ruly, unruly, lawless.

不意 *pu-i*, not intentionally, inadvertently.

不日 *pu-jih*, not a day, *i.e.* before long, shortly.

不時 *pu-shih*, not at (a fixed) time, at irregular hours (as a night-watch controller who has to appear now and then); "at uncertain times."

不等 *pu-têng*, about, more or less; or (*see* paragr. 128 and 129).

不期 *pu-ch'i*, not at the (expected) time, unexpectedly; HOWEVER (202 col. 5).

不料 *pu-liao*, not foreseeing, unexpectedly; HOWEVER (18 col. 8; *cf.* Wade's Note 33).

不過 *pu-kuo*, not exceeding, ONLY (51 col. 3).

不三不四 *pu-san pu-ssŭ*, neither three nor four, neither one thing nor another.

無 *wu*, NOT, NOT HAVING.

(176) The sense of this particle is generally the opposite of 有 *yu*, to have, having; it means *not to have, not having (there is not, there not being)* as may be concluded from numerous cases in which the two words are used antithetically, *e.g.*

無[1] 事[2] 則[3] 互[4] 相[5] 稽[6] 察[7] 有[8] 事[9] 則[10] 一[11] 體[12] 救[13] 援[14]—[1]*wu*-[2]*shih* when you have no case (of robbery) [3]*tsê* then (you should) [6]*chi*-[7]*ch'a* deliberate [4]*hu*-[5]*hsiang* with each other, [8]*yu*-[9]*shih* when you have cases [10]*ts'ê* then (you should) [11]*i*-[12]*t'i* all as a body [13]*chiu*-[14]*yüan* come to the rescue.

"The people should thus prepare against robberies as to

deliberate plans while there are no cases known yet, in order to be able to come to the rescue when attacks are being made" (448; cf. 426 col. 6).

有¹ 益² 無³ 害⁴—¹yu there being ²i advantage ³wu there not being ⁴hai damage; beneficial and not hurtful.

有¹ 名² 無³ 實⁴—¹yu there being ²ming a name ³wu there not being ⁴shih truth, "a name without reality," "a nominal arrangement" (241).

(177) In these senses 無 wu is usually followed by a noun and may often be translated by "without," as in the examples:

病¹ 故² 無³ 嗣⁴—he ¹ping-²ku died from sickness, i.e. he died a natural death ³wu not having, WITHOUT ⁴ssŭ offspring. "He died without children" (183).

老¹ 朽² 無³ 能⁴—¹lao-²hsiu an old piece of rotten wood, a poor old man ³wu not having ⁴nêng strength; " WITHOUT strength" (69).

(178) It occurs also as the prohibitive form of the verb "to have," as in the classical example:

無¹ 友² 不³ 如⁴ 已⁵ 者⁶—¹wu do not have ²yu a friend ⁶chê who is ³pu not ⁴ju like ⁵chi yourself. " You should not have a friend unlike yourself."—Lun-yü, 1. Cf. Marshman p. 481.

身¹ 與² 身³ 妻⁴ 丁⁵ 氏⁶ 永⁷ 無⁸ 異⁹ 言¹⁰—¹shên I ²yü and ³shên-⁴ch'i⁵ my wife ⁵ting-⁶shih née Ting, whose maiden name was Ting, ⁷yung eternally ⁸wu must not have, are not to have ⁹i-¹⁰yen different language. "The contractor and his wife are never to gainsay this agreement" (84).

(179) In the following examples we are bound to consider 無 wu as a verb meaning " not to have" as indicated by the fact of a noun following it:

本¹ 朝² 向³ 無⁴ 全⁵ 權⁶ 大⁷ 臣⁸ 官⁹ 名¹⁰—¹pên-²chao during the present dynasty ³hsiang hitherto ⁴wu we have not had, there has not been ⁹kuan-¹⁰ming the official title of

⁶ch'üan-⁶ch'üan-⁷ta-⁸ch'ên minister plenipotentiary. "No such official designation as that of ch'üan-ch'üan ta-ch'ên, is ever used by the present dynasty" (3).

恐¹ 後² 無³ 憑⁴ 特⁵ 立⁶ 此⁷ 單⁸ 爲⁹ 據¹⁰—¹k'ung fearing that ²hou afterwards ³wu we shall not have, there will not be ⁴p'ing evidence, proof—we ⁵t'ê specially ⁶li draw up ⁷tz'ŭ this ⁸tan document ⁹wei to be, to serve as ¹⁰chü a voucher, proof. "This paper is specially drawn up lest there should be hereafter no proof, etc." (81).

無奈 wu-nai, there is no help for, cannot but.

梁¹ 萬² 和³ 等⁴ 無⁵ 奈⁶ 應⁷ 允⁸—¹liang-²wan-³ho Liang Wan-ho ⁴têng and others ⁵wu-⁶nai had no alternative, could not but ⁷ying-⁸yün agree. "Liang Wan-ho and the rest had nothing for it but to agree to this" [190; cf. 70 col. 2).

(180) 無 wu, may also come to be equivalent to 不 pu, the simple negative before words usually employed as verbs and adjectives.

無許 wu-hsü, not to permit (you have not, there is not permission) (108 cols. 2 and 3).

氏¹ 子² 在³ 港⁴ 朋⁵ 友⁶ 熟⁷ 識⁸ 無⁹ 多¹⁰—of ¹shih the petitioner's (a widow's) ²tzŭ son (there are) ³tsai at ⁴chiang Hong-kong ⁵p'êng-⁶yu friends and ⁷shou-⁸shih acquaintances ⁹wu not ¹⁰to many. "Her son has no great number of friends or intimate acquaintances at Hongkong" (64).

湖¹ 南² 山³ 多⁴ 田⁵ 少⁶ 宜⁷ 稻⁸ 之⁹ 處¹⁰ 無¹¹ 幾¹²—¹hu-²nan of Hunan ³shan hills (being) ⁴to many ⁵t'ien fields (being) ⁶shao few, ¹⁰ch'u places ⁹chih which are ⁷i fit for ⁸tao rice ¹¹wu not (there have not, there are not) ¹²chi many. "As hilly ground abounds and fields are scarce in Hunan, but few places may be adapted to the cultivation of rice" (356).

(181) Note, besides this phrase 無幾 wu chi, "not much," "not many," the following combinations very common in the business style, as well as in general Chinese:

無用 *wu-yung*, of no use, useless.

無論 *wu-lun*, without discussion, no matter whether...or.

無故 *wu-ku*,
無緣 *wu-yüan*, } without cause, groundless.

無辜 *wu-ku*, without guilt, guiltless.

無疑 *wu-i*, without doubt.

無賴 *wu-lai*, without dependence, not to be depended upon.

無常 *wu-ch'ang*, not permanent; not lasting; to die; death.

無能 *wu-néng*, (=不能 *pu-néng*) not able to, cannot.

無名 *wu-ming*, without a name, nameless; also used when the name of an individual (*e.g.* that of a dead body found in the streets) cannot be ascertained: "name unknown."

無所不為 *wu-so-pu-wei*, he does anything; and similar phrases (*cf.* paragr. 94).

非 *fei*, NOT, IS NOT.

(182) As 有 *yu* is the opposite of 無 *wu*, 是 *shih*, to be, must be considered as the opposite of 非 *fei*, not to be (*see* K'ang-hi *s.v.* 非): 實¹ 非² 虛³ 語⁴ ¹*shih* in reality ²*fei* it is not (=不是 *pu-shih*) ³*hsü* empty ⁴*yü* language. "(The notables...) make no unsubstantive allegation" (167). Hence 是非 *shih-fei*, means the rights and wrongs of a case (*cf.* 是是非非, 436 col. 9). It is, however, seldom used in this sense, and may, especially before verbs, be practically considered to have the same force as 不 *pu*, *e.g.*

非敢 *fei-kan*=不敢 *pu-kan*, not to dare.

未 *wei*, NOT, NOT YET.

(183) This particle may in many combinations be considered as the negation of action done, inasmuch as it describes the action of the verb as not done yet, the action done being, in opposition, indicated by 已 *i*, the sign of the past, as the following example will show:

巳¹ 犯² 者³ 毋⁴ 庸⁵ 希⁶ 冀⁷ 未⁸ 犯⁹ 者¹⁰ 宜¹¹ 各¹² 三¹³ 思¹⁴—³ché those who ¹i have ²fan failed against the law ⁴wu-⁵yung need not be anxious ⁶hsi-⁷chi to entertain wishes ¹⁰ché those who ⁸wei have not yet ⁹fan failed ¹¹i should ¹²ko each ¹³san-¹⁴ssŭ consider thrice, ripely consider the matter (439; cf. 173 col. 4; 352 col. 8; 365 col. 11).

184) *Wei*, therefore, often occurs in the meaning "not yet" and is frequently used in such combinations as 尙未 *shang-wei* (194 col. 2); 未曾 *wei-tséng*; 未嘗 *wei-ch'ang*, "not yet," etc. Cf. Rémusat, p. 104.

因¹ 事² 赴³ 陝⁴ 未⁵ 回⁶—he had ¹yin on account of ²shih business ³fu gone to ⁴shan Shensi and ⁵wei not yet ⁶hui returned. "He went on business into Shan Hsi, WHERE HE STILL IS" (69).

至¹ 今² 未³ 放⁴—¹chih till ²chin now ³wei NOT YET ⁴fang released;—"has up to the present time not been released" (10).

Otherwise it may be considered as equivalent to 不 *pu*.

莫 *mo*; 毋 *wu*; 勿 *wu*, NOT, DON'T.

(184) These three particles usually have prohibitive force, the first named, 莫 *mo*, more especially in the colloquial language. Its application in the business style is like that of 不 *pu* or 無 *wu* in the combinations expressing comparison mentioned in paragr. 158.

莫¹ 甚² 於³ 斯⁴—¹mo there is nothing ²shén more intense ³yü than ⁴ssŭ this, "nothing could exceed this."

莫¹ 大² 於³ 天⁴—¹mo there is nothing ¹ta greater ³yü than ⁴t'ien heaven.

莫¹ 大² 之³ 功⁴—⁴kung merits ³chih of which ¹mo there are none ²ta greater, "insurpassable merits"—(Philosinensis).

(185) 毋 *wu* is oftener used as a prohibitive than as a synonym of 無 *wu*, as which, according to K'ang-hsi, it occurs in the *Ku-wén*. In the business style it frequently

occurs in the stereotyped phrase put at the end of proclamations:

毋¹ 違² 特³ 示⁴—²t'ê a special ⁴shih proclamation (which) ¹wu don't, you must not ²wei disobey, "a special proclamation which must not be opposed to"; also in 毋¹ 庸² 議³ ¹wu don't ²yung employ ³i law; "no legal proceedings need be taken,"—a phrase very common in legal documents when parties found not to be guilty are acquitted by the verdict of the court.

(186) 勿 wu, though according to K'ang-hsi a synonym of both 非 fei and 無 wu, chiefly occurs as a prohibitive.

勿¹ 畏² 難³ ¹wu don't ²wei fear ³nan difficulties.

幸¹ 勿² 有³ 緩⁴—¹hsing please ²wu do not ³yu-⁴huan delay; I hope there will be no delay; "at your earliest convenience."

勿¹ 忘² 勿³ 忽⁴ 切⁵ 切⁶ 特⁷ 示⁸—⁵ch'ieh-⁶ch'ieh an important ⁷t'ê special ⁸shih proclamation (which) ¹wu don't ²wang forget and ³wu don't ⁴hu disregard. "Careful attention should be paid to this notice."

非 fu; 否 fou; 罔 wang; 靡 mi.

(187) Of these the first and the last named are but sparingly used; they both correspond to 不 pu, not.

以¹ 弗² 滿³ 其⁴ 職⁵ 是⁶ 憂⁷—¹i because (he had) ²fu not ³man fulfilled ⁴chi his ⁵chih post, the duties of his post ⁶shih therefore ⁷yu he was sad. "Afflicted on account of not having fulfilled the duties of his station" (Philosinensis).

雪¹ 非² 如³ 雨⁴—¹hsüeh snow ²fu is not ³ju like ⁴yü rain, i.e. snow is not so beautiful as rain (Williams), or "rain is better than snow" (非 如 = 不 如; see paragr. 163).

弗 能 fu-nêng, (= 不 能) not able, unable.

弗 克 fu-k'o, inadequate.

弗 知 fu-chih, don't know; it is not known.

天¹ 命² 靡³ 常⁴—¹t'ien-²ming-³mi-⁴ch'ang, the degrees of heaven are not fixed (cf. 371, col. 10).

靡¹ 日² 不³ 思⁴—¹mi-²jih no day (on which he did) ³pu not ⁴ssŭ think of it. "To reflect on it each day" (Williams).

(188) 否 fou implies the negation of a verb to which it is used in opposition in order to express interrogation; it may, therefore, often be translated by "or not."

是¹ 否² 屬³ 實⁴—¹shih is it ²fou or is it not ³shu-⁴shih true. "Is it true?" "Whether it is true" (102).

可¹ 否²—¹k'o-²fou, "can it be done?" "whether it may be done."

未¹ 知² 合³ 否⁴—¹wei-²chih we do not know ³ho-⁴fou whether it is suitable or not (Philosinensis).

否¹ 則² 不³ 誅⁴—¹fou if not, ²ts'ĕ (then) ³pu-⁴chu we shall not kill him (ibid).

(189) 罔 wang, originally "a net," is explained in the Ěrh-ya to be the same as 無 wu. It is a strong negative, almost like the French ne...point.

罔 有 此 事 wang yu tz'ŭ shih there is no such thing (Philosinensis).

GENERAL RULES REGARDING NEGATIVES.

(190) Negative particles are very frequently reinforced by the addition of certain words having no other meaning but to emphasize the negation. The principal characters so employed in the business style are:

並 ping; 斷 tuan; 萬 wan (also 千 ch'ien and 千萬 ch'ien-wan); 毫 hao (also 絲 毫 ssŭ hao); 決 chüeh; 絕 chüeh; 切 ch'ieh; 總 tsung; 終 chung; 迴 ch'iung.

We may translate the negative to which any of these words is prefixed by such expressions as "by no means," "not at all," "not at any rate," but as these combinations are much more frequent in Chinese texts than the strong expressions given here may be conveniently allowed to occur in good English, we may often leave them untranslated.

其¹ 後² 該³ 國⁴ 王⁵ 並⁶ 無⁷ 回⁸ 信⁹—¹ch'i-²hou thereafter

²kai the ⁴kuo-⁵wang King ⁶ping-⁷wu did not ⁸hui-⁹hsin reply. "The King made no reply at all after this" (377).

洋¹ 錢² 並³ 不⁴ 必⁵ 禁⁶—¹yang-²ch'ien foreign coin ⁵pi must ³ping-⁴pu on no account ⁶chin be prohibited (245).

諭¹ 旨² 令³ 各⁴ 該⁵ 督² 撫⁷ 及⁸ 地⁹ 方¹⁰ 等¹¹ 官¹² 出¹³ 具¹⁴ 署¹⁵ 內¹⁶ 並¹⁷ 無¹⁸ 買¹⁹ 食²⁰ 鴉²¹ 片²² 煙²³ 甘²⁴ 結²⁵—¹yü-²chih an Imperial edict ³ling orders, causes ⁵kai the ⁶tu-⁷fu viceroys and governors ⁸chi and ⁹ti-¹⁰fang local ¹¹têng and other ¹²kuan mandarins ¹³ch'u-¹⁴ch'ü to prepare, sign ²⁴kan-²⁵chi a bond that ¹⁵shu-¹⁶nei within their yamêns ¹⁷ping-¹⁸wu there is really no ¹⁹mai-²⁰shih buying or smoking of ²¹ya-²²pien-²³yen opium. "An Imperial order requires the various viceroys and governors, together with the local and other officials, to sign a bond to the effect that no opium is either bought or smoked within the limits of their Yamêns" (296; cf. 244 col. 12; 245 col. 1; 295 col. 3; 292 col. 1; etc).

但¹ 求² 有³ 益⁴ 於⁵ 地⁶ 方⁷ 斷⁸ 不⁹ 固¹⁰ 執¹¹ 乎¹² 己¹³ 見¹⁴—I ¹tan only ²ch'iu seek to ³yu-⁴i be of advantage ⁵yü to ⁶ti-⁷fang the country; ⁸tuan-⁹pu and not by any means ¹⁰ku-¹¹chih keep obstinate hold or "stick" ¹²hu to ¹³chi my own ¹⁴chien view. "His (the writer's) only object is the good of the prefecture; he will certainly not adhere with tenacity to any view because it is his own" (108).

有¹ 案² 必³ 須⁴ 速⁵ 報⁶ 已⁷ 報⁸ 必⁹ 須¹⁰ 卽¹¹ 破¹² 斷¹³ 不¹⁴ 可¹⁵ 苟¹⁶ 安¹⁷ 粉¹⁸ 飾¹⁹—¹yu-²an if there be a case, ³pi-⁴hsü it must be ⁵su speedily ⁶pao reported; ⁷i-⁸pao having been reported ⁹pi-¹⁰hsü it must be ¹¹ch'i quickly ¹²po investigated; ¹³tuan-¹⁴pu ¹⁵k'o it cannot, must not by any means be ¹⁶kao-¹⁷an carelessly ¹⁸fên-¹⁹shih whitewashed. "All cases arising should be at once reported and then promptly dealt with; a careless sham-settlement should not by any means be allowed" (375).

鬧¹ 事² 斷³ 非⁴ 我⁵ 輩⁶ 所⁷ 爲⁸—³tuan-⁴fei (it was) really not ⁵wo-⁶pei our class, we ⁷so who ⁸wei made ¹nao-²shih the trouble. "The trouble was indeed not made by us" (325).

如¹ 有² 前³ 項⁴ 情⁵ 事⁶ 立⁷ 卽⁸ 治⁹ 以¹⁰ 軍¹¹ 法¹² 萬¹³ 勿¹⁴ 稍¹⁵ 有¹⁶ 姑¹⁷ 息¹⁸—¹ju if ²yu there are ⁵ch'ing-⁶shih matters, cases of ³ch'ien-⁴hsiang the before (mentioned) kind, they are ⁷li-⁸chi at once ⁹chih to be punished ¹⁰i by ¹¹chün-¹²fa military law; there will ¹³wan-¹⁴wu by no means ¹⁵shao in the least ¹⁶yu be ¹⁷ku-¹⁸hsi indulgence. "If (soldiers, police, or train-band men) do the things above enumerated, let them be punished at once by military law; let them be shewn no indulgence whatever" (102; cf. 370 col. 8; 360 col. 4).

吾¹ 弟² 務³ 須⁴ 迅⁵ 速⁶ 言⁷ 旋⁸ 千⁹ 萬¹⁰ 不¹¹ 必¹² 久¹³ 留¹⁴—¹wu-²ti my younger brother, i.e. you ³wu-⁴hsü must ⁵hsün-⁶su quickly ⁷yen-⁸hsüan return an answer, and ¹²pi must ⁹ch'ien-¹⁰wan ¹¹pu by no means, on no account ¹³chiu-¹⁴liu hold on a long time (334).

該¹ 州² 縣³ 會⁴ 同⁵ 各⁶ 委⁷ 員⁸ 實⁹ 心¹⁰ 查¹¹ 辦¹² 毫¹³ 不¹⁴ 擾¹⁵ 累¹⁶ 民¹⁷ 家¹⁸—¹kai the respective ²chou-³hsien Chou and Hsien Magistrates ⁴hui-⁵t'ung conjointly with ⁶ko ⁷wei-⁸yüan the Deputies ⁹shih-¹⁰hsin true heartedly ¹¹ch'a-¹²pan investigated, and ¹³hao-¹⁴pu by no means ¹⁵yu-¹⁶lei implicated in trouble ¹⁷min-¹⁸chia the families of the people. "The magistrates of districts, major and minor, and the officers sent by the High Authorities have co-operated together, and the fidelity with which they have prosecuted their enquiries and taken action (has) in no way disturbed or embarrassed the people" (106 cf. 369 col. 10; 101 col. 4).

(191) A double negative amounts to a strong affirmation; the same may be said of a negative particle entering into combination with a verb of negative meaning, as 未免 wei-mien, not to avoid, i.e. to be bound to.

遇¹有²與³該⁴省⁵地⁶方⁷官⁸書⁹信¹⁰往¹¹來¹²無¹³不¹⁴以¹⁵彈¹⁶壓¹⁷地¹⁸方¹⁹爲²⁰囑²¹—¹yü happening ²yu to be, *i.e.* whenever there happened to be ⁹*shu*-¹⁰*hsin* correspondence ⁸*yü* with ⁶*ti*-⁷*fang*-⁸*kuan* the local officials of ⁴*kai*-⁵*shêng* that province ¹¹*wang*-¹²*lai* coming and going, ¹³*wu*-¹⁴*pu* ²⁰*wei* he does not not make, *i.e.* he invariably makes ¹⁵*i* (sign of the object) ¹⁶*t'an*-¹⁷*ya* ¹⁸*ti*-¹⁹*fang* the keeping in order of the country ²¹*shu* an enjoinment. "In his correspondence with the authorities of that place, he (the Commissioner) never fails to enjoin them to maintain order" (18).

罔¹不²周³知⁴—¹*wang* not ²*pu*-³*chou*-⁴*chih* not known; not unknown, *i.e.* it is very well known (58).

從¹前²乾³隆⁴嘉⁵慶⁶年⁷間⁸挖⁹災¹⁰冒¹¹賑¹²之¹³案¹⁴無¹⁵不¹⁶盡¹⁷法¹⁸處¹⁹治²⁰—¹*ts'ung*-²*ch'ien* formerly ⁷*nien*-⁸*chien* during the years, during the reign of ³*chien*-⁴*lung* ⁵*chia*-⁶*ch'ing* the Emperors Kien-lung and Kia-king ¹⁴*an* cases ¹³*chih* of ⁹*nieh* feigning ¹⁰*tsai* a calamity, and ¹¹*mao* obtaining by false pretences ¹²*chên* public charity ¹⁵*wu*-¹⁶*pu* were ALWAYS ¹⁷*chin*-¹⁸*fa* with the full severity of the law ¹⁹*ch'u*-²⁰*chih* punished. "At the time of Kien-lung and Kia-king no cases of obtaining public funds under the false pretext of a calamity having befallen a district were allowed to escape punishment, all being dealt with by the full severity of the law" (263; *cf.* 196 col. 4).

未¹免²累³及⁴保⁵人⁶—¹*wei* not ²*mien* to avoid, *i.e.* is sure to, is bound to ³*lei*-⁴*chi* involve ⁵*pao*-⁶*jên* the guarantee. "[His failure will] inevitably involve his securities" (56).*

斷¹無²不³惜⁴其⁵身⁶家⁷性⁸命⁹—¹*tuan*-²*wu* there is indeed no such thing as ³*pu*-⁴*hsi* not regarding ⁸*hsing*-⁹*ming*

* Two terms of negative meaning may produce a similar affirmative sense, as 難免 *nan-mien* in the following example: 壩¹下²田³畝⁴難⁵免⁶被⁷淹³—¹*pa*-²*hsia* ³*t'ien*-⁴*mou* the fields below the embankment ⁵*nan*-⁶*mien* will hardly avoid, will scarcely escape ⁷*pei*-⁸*yen* being overflooded. "The fields below the embankment are very liable to inundation" (257).

the life of ^{6}shên-^{7}chia one's people. "The life of their own people is cared for above everything" (271).

無 日 不 wu-jih pu, there is no day on which not...i.e. "every day."

無 歲 不 wu-sui pu, every year (270 col. 9 ; 353 col. 4).

(192) Such phrases as 不可不 pu-k'o-pu, 不能不 pu-nêng-pu, etc., are translatable by, say, "cannot but," "must," "is bound to," or some similar expression corresponding to the Latin "facere non posse quin."

不^1 可^2 不^3 查^4 詢^5 明^6 確^7 以^8 防^9 弊^{10} 混^{11}—^{1}pu-^{2}k'o we cannot ^{3}pu but ^{4}ch'a-^{5}hsün investigate ^{6}ming-^{7}ch'io the truth ^{8}i in order to ^{9}fang ward off ^{10}p'i-^{11}hun malpractices. "The affair must be thoroughly investigated, in order to the prevention of frauds and malpractices" (28 ; cf. 349 col. 5).

(193) Chinese writers like to substitute an interrogative clause for a simple negative, as if we were to say: "How could I," instead of "I could not;" or "who does" instead of "nobody does" (or "who does not" instead of "everybody does"), etc.

民^1 困^2 獲^3 甦^4 豈^5 可^6 添^7 此^8 累^9 民^{10} 累^{11} 官^{12} 之^{13} 事^{14}—^{1}min-^{2}k'un ^{3}hu-^{4}su as the people are greatly suffering: —^{5}cni-^{6}k'o how could we ^{7}tien add ^{8}tz'ŭ this ^{14}shih matter ^{13}chih which ^{9}lei implicates (in trouble) ^{10}min the people and ^{11}lei implicates ^{12}kuan the mandarins, i.e. "we should NOT introduce a measure crossing the interests of both the people and the authorities" (357 ; cf. 109 col. 9).

其^1 慘^2 目^3 傷^4 心^5 可^6 勝^7 道^8 耶^9—^{1}ch'i of it ^{2}ts'an-^{3}mu the offending the eye and ^{4}shang-^{5}hsin the wounding the heart, ^{6}k'o-^{7}shêng-^{8}tao can it be told ^{9}yeh (interrogative particle)? or : "so cruel and heartrending a sight it is not possible to describe" (318 ; cf. 320 col. 12).

災^1 賑^2 重^3 務^4 就^5 敢^6 徇^7 庇^8 姑^9 容^{10}—^{1}tsai-^{2}chên the relief of calamitous (districts) ^{3}chung-^{4}wu being very important ⁵shu-⁶kan who dares to ⁷hsün-⁸pi stand up for the underserving and ⁹ku-¹⁰yung take it easy? "The relief of calamitous districts is a matter of grave importance of which nobody would dare to make a trifling matter by standing up for the undeserving" (271).

(194) This must be looked upon as a rhetorical feature of the language rather than as a grammatical one. Another peculiarity, in which negative particles are frequently employed, is the predilection many writers have for antithetical phrases, *i.e.* compound expressions, in which the same idea appears twice, once in its positive, and once in its negative form. This is also a mere mannerism which need not be expressed in an English translation, *e.g.*

推¹諉²不³認⁴—¹t'ui-²wei to back out ³pu-⁴jên and not admit "to evade one's responsibilities and deny one's acts" (18).

因¹ 事² 赴³ 陝⁴ 未⁵ 回⁶—¹yin-²shih on account of business (he had) ³fu gone to ⁴shan Shensi and ⁵wei-⁶hui not returned. "He had gone to Shensi on business, and not come back yet" (69).

吳¹ 瓦² 藏³ 匿⁴ 不⁵ 見⁶—¹wu-²liang Wu-Liang ³ts'ang-⁴ni concealed himself ⁵pu-⁶chien and was not to be seen (69).

伊¹ 視² 身³ 老⁴ 朽⁵ 無⁶ 能⁷—¹i he ²shih saw ³shên me (being) ⁴lao-⁵hsiu old and rotten and ⁶wu-⁷nêng having no power. "Seeing that petitioner was a broken old man of no strength" (69).

賴¹ 帳² 不³ 還⁴—¹lai-²chang to take advantage of a debt, *i.e.* not to pay a debt, and ³pu-⁴huan not return the money. "To repudiate a debt," "to maliciously refuse payment" (75; *cf.* 226 col. 5).

怙¹ 惡² 不³ 悛⁴ 之⁵ 土⁶ 匪⁷ 等⁸—⁶t'u-⁷fei-⁸têng local outlaws ⁵chih who ¹hu-²ngo rely on wickedness and ³pu-⁴chüan do not change. "Outlaws wickedly obdurate and irredeemable" (103).

Adverbs.

(195) Apart from such words which from the nature of their meaning cannot be classified but as adverbs, such as 今 *chin* (now), every noun, or every compound expression based upon a noun, may take the place of what we would call an adverb or an adverbial phrase by being placed before a verb. When the subject is not specially mentioned, but implied in the verb, it is in such cases often difficult to distinguish between a noun representing the subject and a noun taking the place of an adverb. 明¹ 日² 不³ 來⁴, grammatically, may mean ¹*ming*-²*jih* the following day, the morrow (subject) ³*pu*-⁴*lai* does not come, has not come; but common sense will force us in this case (as the general context in others) to look at ¹*ming*-²*jih* as an adverbial expression meaning "to-morrow."

所¹ 有² 查³ 明⁴ 江⁵ 蘇⁶ 地⁷ 方⁸ 現⁹ 無¹⁰ 種¹¹ 鴉¹² 片¹³ 煙¹⁴ 緣¹⁵ 由¹⁶—At ¹*so*-²*yu* the ⁷*ti*-⁸*fang* places ³*ch'a*-⁴*ming* examined ⁹*hsien*-¹⁰*wu* there are now no ¹⁵*yüan*-¹⁶*yu* cases of ¹¹*chung* planting ¹²*ya*-¹³*p'ien*-¹⁴*yen* Opium. "No Opium is now grown in the districts examined" (238).

We would be quite justified to translate: "the places examined (subject) now do not grow opium," as the noun (⁷*ti*-⁸*fang*) may from its position be either subject *or* adverb, and in this case either translation would give a similar sense, whereas in many cases common sense will exclude either the one or the other, as in:

該¹ 地² 之³ 土⁴ 人⁵ 無⁶ 種⁷ 鴉⁸ 片⁹ 煙¹⁰ 緣¹¹ 由¹²—¹*kai*-²*ti*-³*chih* ⁴*t'u*-⁵*jên* the natives of that place ⁶*wu*-⁷*chung* ⁸*ya*-⁹*p'ien* ¹⁰*yen* ¹¹*yüan*-¹²*yu* do not grow Opium, and,

光¹ 緒² 元³ 年⁴ 無⁵ 種⁶ 鴉⁷ 片⁸ 煙⁹ 緣¹⁰ 由¹¹—¹*kuang*-²*hsü* ³*yüan* ⁴*nien* during the first year of Kuang-hsü ⁵*wu*-⁶*chung* ⁷*ya* ⁸*p'ien*-⁹*yen* ⁰¹*yüan*¹¹*yu* they (subject implied in verb) grew no opium.

Adverbs of Time.

(196) The Dictionary contains a great many words which, according to their use, may be considered as adverbs of some of the categories commonly adopted in general grammar. We have already dealt with Negatives, which we might have called adverbs of negation, and propose to now enumerate some of the adverbs of time commonly used in the business style.

"Now" is expressed by 今 *chin*, 現 *hsien*, 茲 *tzŭ*; also by compound terms like 現在 *hsien-tsai*; 現今 *hsien-chin*, etc.; the present time is also involved in expressions like 今日 *chin-jih*, the present day, to-day; 今年 *chin-nien*, 本年 *pên-nien*, the present year. The simple particle is, especially at the beginning of a sentence, often followed by 者 *chê*, as in 今者 *chin-chê*, or 茲者 *tzŭ-chê*, both of which mean "now;" 是時 *shih-shih* means at that time, at the same time; 是日 *shih-jih*, on that day, on the same day.

時 *shih*, alone, means "at the time" (176 col. 12; 199 col. 3); 不時 *pu-shih*, on the other hand, is used to denote that the time at which an action is done is not regular: it means "at no fixed time," "at irregular hours" (*cf.* p. 126 of these notes).

委[1] 官[3] 不[3] 時[4] 抽[5] 查[6]—[1]*wei*-[2]*kuan* deputies (will) [3]*pu*-[4]*shih* at irregular times, from time to time [5]*ch'ou-ch'a* pick out and examine (the census tickets—mentioned before in the text). "Officers will be sent from time to time to examine a ticket here and a ticket there" (111).

不[1] 日[2] *pu-jih*, in no time, shortly:

昨[1] 接[2] 來[3] 函[4] 知[5] 貴[6] 大[7] 臣[8] 不[9] 日[10] 榮[11] 旋[12]—I [1]*tso* yesterday [2]*chieh* received [3]*lai*-[4]*han* a coming cover, a note [5]*chih* informing (me that) [6]*kuei*-[7]*ta*-[8]*ch'ên* you, the Minister [9]*pu*-[10]*jih* very shortly [11]*jung*-[12]*hsüan* will return home.

"[The writer] received a note from His Excellency yesterday, informing him that he should be going home almost immediately " (42).

時·時 shih-shih, at all times, always, constantly.

先時 hsien-shih
昔時 hsi-shih } formerly.

此時 tz‘ŭ-shih, at this time.

當時 t‘ang-shih (=是時 shih-shih), at that time, at the same time.

後時 hou-shih, in future, afterwards.

隨時 sui-shih, afterwards, in the sequel, then.

於時 yü-shih, thereupon.

有時 yŭ-shih, sometimes.

何時 ho-shih, at what time ? when ?

早 tsao, early, soon (蚤 tsao, "flea," is sometimes substituted for this character).

久 chiu, 已久 i-chiu, long ago.

古 ku, 古者 ku-chê, of old.

近 chin, 近日 chin-jih, recently, lately, (18 col. 8 "a short time since," Wade).

向 hsiang, 向來 hsiang-lai, hitherto.

往日 wang-jih, 昔 hsi, 昔日 hsi-jih, 昔者 hsi-chê, formerly.

終日 chung-jih, all day.

終年 chung-nien, all the year round, but 於年終 yü nien-chung, at the end of the year (239 col. 9).

嗣 ssŭ, 嗣後 ssŭ-hou, in future, henceforward (245 col. 11).

其後 ch‘i-hou, thereafter.

前 chien, before; 後 hou, afterwards.

至今 chih-chin, up to the present, "adhuc." The same meaning attaches to 迄今 hsi-chin.

迄¹今²未³准⁴移⁵到⁶—¹hsi-²chin up to the present,

DOCUMENTARY STYLE. 141

³*wei* did not ⁴*chun* receive ⁵⁻⁶*tao* the arrival of the despatch. "No reply has as yet reached the Prefect" (100).

先後 *hsien-hou*, before and after; severally, repeatedly, at various times, etc.

續¹據²稟³獲⁴張⁵貴⁶等⁷先⁸後⁹共¹⁰獲¹¹犯¹²八¹³十¹⁴二¹⁵名¹⁶—¹*hsü* further ²*chü* according to ³*ping* a petition, a report ⁴*hu* they has seized ⁵*chang* ⁶*kuei* Chang Kuei ⁷*téng* and others, and had ⁸*hsien*-⁹*hou* at various times ¹⁰*kung* in all ¹¹*hu* seized ¹³*pa*-¹⁴*shih*-¹⁵*êrh* eighty-two ¹⁶*ming* men; "—he subsequently received a report of the arrest of Chang Kuei and other persons, eighty-two in all, who had been taken, some of them earlier and some later" (205; *cf.* 27 col. 6; 36 col. 5; 173 col. 2).

ADVERBS OF PLACE.

(197) Such adverbs are often formed by the prefixing of 在 *tsai*, as in 在此 *tsai-tz'ŭ*, here, or 在彼 *tsai-pi*, there; *tz'ŭ* and *pi* are also used without *tsai*.

梁¹萬²和³訛⁴聞⁵蘇⁶萬⁷全⁸弟⁹兄¹⁰—¹¹同¹²在¹³彼¹⁴起¹⁵意¹⁶捉¹⁷孥¹⁸送¹⁹官²⁰—¹*liang*-²*wan*-³*ho* Liang Wan-ho ⁴*ngo*-⁵*wên* having heard by mistake that ⁶*su*-⁷*wan*-⁸*ch'üan* Su Wan-ch'üan and ⁹*ti*-¹⁰*hsiung* his elder and younger brother ¹¹*i*-¹²*t'ung* together with him ¹³*tsai*-¹⁴*pi* were THERE ¹⁵*ch'i*-¹⁶*i* he conceived the idea ¹⁷*cho*-¹⁸*na* to seize him and ¹⁹*sung*-²⁰*kuan* send him to the Mandarin. "Liang Wan-ho had been informed by mistake that he was there as well as his elder and younger brother, and this suggested to him the idea of pouncing upon Su Wan-ch'üan and delivering him up to justice" (191; *cf.* 126 col. 10; 到彼 *tao-pi*, to arrive there).

彼此 *pi-tz'ŭ*, meaning "here and there," or "on either side," etc., has been mentioned on p. 78.

ADVERBS OF QUALITY.

(198) As such we may consider combinations like 似此

ssŭ-tz'ŭ, *lit.* like this, *i.e.* "thus"; or 如此 *jn-tz'ŭ*, 如是 *ju-shih*, etc., having the same meaning.

似¹ 此² 製³ 賣⁴ 處⁵ 所⁶ 一⁷ 切⁸ 與⁹ 例¹⁰ 無¹¹ 礙¹²—¹*ssŭ*-²*tz'ŭ* like this, thus ³*chi*-⁴*mai*-⁵*chu*-⁶*so* [as regards] the places of manufacture and sale ⁷*i*-⁸*ch'ieh* [there is] throughout ¹¹*wu*-¹²*ai* no difficulty ⁹*yü*-¹⁰*li* with the law. "There is nothing, therefore, either in the place of its manufacture, or in the place of its sale, that is in non-accordance with the law" (57; *cf.* 54 col. 7; 398 col. 12; 245 col. 5).

可¹ 以² 如³ 此⁴ 辦⁵ 理⁶—A matter ¹*ko*-²*i* may be ⁵*pan*-⁶*li* managed ³*ju*-⁴*tz'ŭ* like this, thus (379).

有¹ 難² 爲³ 吾⁴ 弟⁵ 言⁶ 者⁷ 卽⁸ 吾⁹ 弟¹⁰ 亦¹¹ 必¹² 不¹³ 能¹⁴ 料¹⁵ 有¹⁶ 如¹⁷ 是¹⁸ 之¹⁹ 苦²⁰—¹*yu* if there are ²*nan* difficulties ³*wei* ⁶*yen* ⁷*chê* which are to be told by ⁴*wu*-⁵*ti* my brother, *i.e.* you, or your good self ⁸*ch'i* [then] ⁹*wu*-¹⁰*ti* you ¹²*pi* must, could ¹¹*yeh* also ¹³*pu*-¹⁴*nêng* not be able to ¹⁵*liao* foresee ¹⁶*yu* that there would be ¹⁷*ju*-¹⁸*shih* like this, such ¹⁹*chih* [marking genitive] ²⁰*k'u* troubles. "The difficulties you mention are of such a kind that you could not possibly foresee there would be any such trouble" (341)*

若輩 *jo-pei*, *lit.* of this class, like this, is sometimes equivalent to 如此 *ju-tz'ŭ*, meaning "thus," "of such sort" [*cf.* Williams' *Syll. Dict.*, p. 296].

往¹ 住² 若³ 輩⁴ 爲⁵ 之⁶—⁵*wei* they do ⁶*chih* it ¹*wang*-²*wang* frequently ³*jo*-⁴*pei* like this; "it is often so" (266).

ADVERBS OF QUANTITY.

(199) Some of these have been spoken of on p. 88 in connection with the superlative degree of comparison, *viz.*, 最 *tsui*, 極 *chi*, 甚 *shên*, etc., all of which may be looked at as adverbs inasmuch as they qualify the sense of an adjective. Some comparative particles, as 更 *kêng* and 尤 *yu* (see p.

---

* 如是 *ju-shih* is here, by its position, to be looked at as an adjective rather than an adverb.

116 *seq.*) may also be brought under this head. 較 *chiao*,-otherwise the comparative particle corresponding to the Latin *quam*, is quite commonly used as an adverb of quantity before adjectives in the sense of "somewhat," "rather."

因¹ 贛² 郡³ 距⁴ 省⁵ 較⁶ 遠⁷—¹*yin* because ²*kan*-³*chün* the Kan district (is) ⁶*chiao* somewhat, rather ⁷*yüan* distant ⁴*chü* from ⁵*shêng* the provincial capital (205).

A similar meaning attaches to 頗 *p'o* and 稍 *shao*, 頗多 *p'o-to*, 稍多 *shao-to*, rather much.

粵¹ 省² 入³ 夏⁴ 以⁵ 來⁶ 雨⁷ 水⁸ 稍⁹ 多¹⁰—¹*yüeh*-²*shêng* in the province of Yüeh (=Kuang-tung) ³*ju*-⁴*hsia* ⁵*i*-⁶*lai* since the beginning of the summer ⁷*yü*-⁸*shui* rain water (was) ⁹*shao*-¹⁰*to* rather much. "Rainfalls have been unusually heavy in the Canton province during the summer" (430).

The peculiar position of some of these words has been commented upon on p. 121 *seqq*. (*cf*. the position of 多 *to* in Note 153, p. 115).

Prepositions.

在 *tsai*, and 於 *yü*.

(200) 在 *tsai* is the principal local preposition, in which sense it occurs much more frequently than in that of the verb "to be," the original meaning.

在 虎 門 寨—AT Hu-mên-chai (14).

在 該 處—AT the said place (193).

在 監 病 故—He died IN jail (294).

在 此 *tsai-tz'ŭ* here; 在 彼 *tsai-p'i* there.

船 在 香 港 海 面 遇 有 熟 識 鄭 全 與 小 料 船 在 此 灣 泊 領 照—"The vessel being in the Hongkong waters, his friend fell in with a small vessel belonging to an old acquaintance by name Chêng Ch'üan-hsing, which was at anchor IN the same place" (59).

在 番 IN foreign countries; abroad (319 col. 10).

在 何 處 AT what place? where?

載在條約—It is stated IN the Treaty (Williams).

在案 *tsai-an*, IN the records; ON record; IS ON record. This phrase is often found at the end of quotations of passages or statements of facts mentioned in official documents; it is added in order to show that the facts mentioned have been entered in the records and cannot be gainsaid. Such quotations of passages or statements of facts are a sort of recapitulation of the principal phases of a case in hand, and constitute, so to speak, the preamble of a despatch, which is followed by the subject proper, often introduced by 查 *ch'a*, 茲 *tzŭ*, 茲查 *tzŭ-ch'a*, "now," "it must now be stated that," *e.g.* "your despatch, in which you state that, etc., *tsai-an*, being on record, *tzŭ-ch'a*, it must now be stated that, etc." Examples abound in all classes of documents (*See* 4 col. 9; 6 col. 1; 11 col. 3; etc.)

This preposition is often combined with words commonly used as postpositions, such as 中 *chung*, 內 *nei*, 外 *wai*, 上 *shang*, 面 *mien*, etc.

在水中 IN the water; under water.

在城外 outside the city; in the suburbs.

在內 *tsai-nei* and 在外 *tsai-wai*, stand for "inner" and "outer;" "to be included;" "inclusive" and "exclusive."

不在內 "not including;" "exclusive of" [what precedes this phrase].

在當面 before one's face; in one's presence.

於 *yü*, in the sense of a local preposition, is a synonym of 在 *tsai*, with which it is sometimes combined, as in 在於水中 IN the water, under water.

於該處 AT the said place.

於滇 IN the Yünnan province (347 col. 8).

於左 ON the left, *i.e.* what we would call "below" in documents.

今¹ 將² 公³ 議⁴ 各⁵ 例⁶ 列⁷ 於⁸ 左⁹—we ¹*chin* now ⁷*lieh*

enumerate, state ²*chiang*, [introducing the object] ³*kung*-⁴*i* ⁵*ko*-⁶*li* the by-laws agreed upon ⁸*yü*-⁹*ts'o* on the left, *i.e.* on the space following on the left; "below" (405). *Cf.* 右照會 *lit.* the despatch on the right, "the preceding despatch," "the above despatch" (4).

The combining with a preposition of words used as postpositions is still more common with 於 *yü* than it is with 在 *tsai*.

於條約之內 "in the treaty."

於稔收處所 at the places where the crop was taken in (263).

於 *yü* is also very commonly used as a preposition of time.

於同治元年 IN the first year of T'ung-chih.

於日出之時 AT the time of sunrise.

After an adjective, 於 *yü* usually has comparative force, and corresponds to "than."

水高於岸 the water was higher *than* the shore, *i.e.* "the water overflowed," and not, "the water reached up to the shore," as one might be tempted to translate (334 col. 11).

滇中之利莫大於銅 of the advantages of the Yünnan province none is larger *than* copper, *i.e.* "copper is the principal source of wealth in Yünnan."

One of the principal functions performed by this preposition appears to be the force it possesses to place a verb in the passive mood, when following. It then corresponds to Latin *a* or *ab* cum ablativo.

殺其父 he killed his father.

殺於其父 he was killed BY his father.

於 *yü* helps to produce in a verb the force of the Latin Supine after terms involving the meaning of difficulty or easiness, such as 難 *nan*, hard, 易 *i*, easy, 足 *tsu*, sufficient, etc. In this sense it may be interchanged with 以 *i*.

易於上岸 easy TO land (359).

難於搭運 there is difficulty in forwarding (355).

愚民易於圖終難於慮始—"with the common people speculation as to the end is easy, but forethoughtful consideration of the beginning, difficult" (105).

田園不足於耕—fields and gardens not sufficient FOR ploughing; "there is not enough land for agriculture" (317).

www.ingramcontent.com/pod-product-compliance
Lightning Source LLC
Chambersburg PA
CBHW030332170426
43202CB00010B/1105